ENVISIONING
equity

Educating and Graduating Low-income,
First-generation, and Minority College Students

Angela Provitera McGlynn

Atwood Publishing
Madison, Wisconsin

Envisioning Equity: Educating and Graduating Low-income, First-generation, and Minority College Students
By Angela Provitera McGlynn

ISBN: 978-1-891859-84-7

© 2011, Atwood Publishing, www.atwoodpublishing.com
Printed in the United States of America.

Cover design by Tamara Dever, TLC Graphics, www.tlcgraphics.com
Chapter header design by Christopher Cameron Scott
Author photo by Katharine Scott

Library of Congress Cataloging-in-Publication Data

Provitera-McGlynn, Angela
    Envisioning equity : educating and graduating low-income, first-generation, and minority college students / by Angela Provitera McGlynn.
        p. cm.
    Includes bibliographical references and index.
    ISBN 978-1-891859-84-7 (pb)
        1. Postsecondary education—United States. 2. Educational equalization—United States. 3. College graduates—United States 4. People with social disabilities—Education (Higher)—United States. 5. First-generation college students—United States. 6. Minority college students—United States. 7. Minorities—Education (Higher)—United States. I. Title.
    LC1039.5.P76 2011
    378.1'9820973—dc23
                    2011019545

ACKNOWLEDGMENTS

Special Thanks To...

BRUCE McGLYNN, my loving, kind, and funny husband who is my sounding board for many ideas and who has contributed immensely to my well-being in life

ANN PROVITERA, my mom, whose loving nurturance all through my life has supported me

JOSEPH PROVITERA, my dad, now deceased, who taught me the value of education and life-long learning by modeling it

CHRISTOPHER SCOTT for his chapter heading designs; KATHARINE SCOTT for the book jacket photograph, and both Christopher and Katharine for lighting up my life

RANDI and DAVID SCOTT for sharing their unconditional love

LINDA BABLER, publisher of Atwood Publishing, for her continuing contributions to the education discussion, for her encouragement to pursue this book, for her support of my work, and for her valuable feedback on the manuscript

TAMARA DEVER, president of TLC Graphics, for her creative and beautiful design of the jacket cover

JILLIAN POTTER, for her great editorial work on this project

WILLIAM CODY for his editorial expertise

PHYLLIS ANGELONI, my cousin who supports everything I try in life, for always being there for me

NIDIA STONE, my long-time precious friend, for our on-going conversations about life

BOB ROSANIA, the brother I never had, Vera Regoli, and Aaron for their nurturing friendship

KATHY FEDORKO, my decades long breakfast partner and cherished friend, for talking to me about teaching and learning all through the years

MARILYN GILROY, my supportive friend, for her mentoring of my writing and her loyalty to our tennis game

RAY and MARILYN STARKER, for their life-long and loving friendship

All the colleges and universities that have invited me to present, and to their faculty participants who have enriched my perspective on education

George Colnaghi, Patricia Carr, Bill Engler, Linda Bregstein Scherr, Fran Davidson, Gianna Dorso-Finley, Bonnie Warren Cohen, Len Sciorra, Patricia Ranft Pollitt, Marianne Reynolds, and all my Mercer County Community College colleagues for their treasured friendship and contributions to my thinking about education

Table of Contents

Introduction: Why I Wrote this Book

Since 1997, I have been a regular contributor to *The Hispanic Outlook in Higher Education*, a publication that has contributed immensely to our understanding of the plight of underserved students in our colleges and universities. Much of my writing has been aimed at analyzing the latest reports on issues related to low-income, first-generation, and minority students.

From 1971 to 2006, I taught at Mercer County Community College in central New Jersey, where I was struck with the diversity of students in my classes—not only in terms of race/ethnicity and country of origin, but also in terms of preparation for college-level work. There were great differences among my students, with some coming from middle-class backgrounds and excellent high schools, and others from less privileged backgrounds. I felt challenged to help more of my students, especially the those from poorer backgrounds, become academically successful.

For more than a decade, I have been doing presentations and workshops about teaching and learning, both in the community college sector and for private and public colleges and universities. These visits to all types of higher education institutions have shown me that the issues of teaching and learning are basically the same all over, with faculty striving for more effective ways to reach their students, particularly those in the age group we call Millennials.

In my travels around the country, I have met college leaders—presidents, academic vice presidents, provosts, and deans—who share similar objectives with their faculties: they want to promote academic success for many different types of student.

So I conceived of a book that incorporates some of the latest thinking and research that might help us achieve this goal. Given America's changing demographic makeup and its place in a competitive global economy, I believe we need to do a much better job of providing excellent higher education to a wider segment of the population. We need to do this because it is the right thing for the underserved and is crucial for the wellbeing of our nation.

A Word About Language

This book will employ the following terms according to their common usage:

Hispanic and Latino(a) are used to describe peoples in our nation who come from a host of different countries. The terms will be used interchangeably throughout this book. "Hispanic" is generally perceived as more generic, since "Latino" (masculine) and "Latina" (feminine) are associated with peoples primarily originating from Latin American countries. Unless the text specifically refers to female people, "Latino" will be used as the indeterminate, describing both males and females, notwithstanding recognition of its exclusionary structure.

Hispanic-Serving Institutions (HSIs) are defined as colleges, universities, or systems/districts where Hispanic enrollment constitutes a minimum of 25% of total enrollment. They are public or private, nonprofit, degree-granting institutions, and are funded based on the Higher Education Opportunity Act of 2008.

The HSI Program provides grants to help HSIs expand educational opportunities for, and improve the attainment of, Hispanic students. HSI Program grants also enable HSIs to extend and enhance their academic offerings, program quality, and institutional stabilit.. (U.S. Department of Education, Ed/Gov at: http://www2.ed.gov/program.)

The terms *African American* and *Black* will be used to describe people of color in America who have their family origins in Africa or the Caribbean Islands. The terms will be used interchangeably. "Black" seems more inclusive than "African American" since many American Blacks do not see their origins as African. Others prefer the term "people of color" over either "African American" or "Black" since it is even more inclusive.

Minority Group: A minority is a sociological group that does not make up a politically dominant voting majority of the total population of a given society. A sociological minority is not necessarily a numerical minority — it may include any group that is subnor-

9

mal with respect to a dominant group in terms of social status, education, employment, wealth, and political power. To avoid confusion, some writers prefer the terms "subordinate group" and "dominant group" rather than "minority" and "majority," respectively. In socioeconomics, the term "minority" typically refers to a socially subordinate ethnic group (understood in terms of language, nationality, religion, and/or culture). Other minority groups include people with disabilities, "economic minorities" (working poor or unemployed), "age minorities" (who are younger or older than a typical working age), and sexual minorities.

The term "minority group" often appears within the discourse of civil rights and collective rights that gained prominence in the twentieth century. Members of minority groups are prone to different (i.e., discriminatory) treatment in the countries and societies in which they live. This discrimination may be directly based on people's perceived membership in a minority group, without consideration of those people's individual achievements. It may also occur indirectly, due to social structures that are not equally accessible to all. Activists campaigning on a range of issues may use the language of minority rights, including student rights, consumer rights, and animal rights. In recent years, some members of social groups traditionally perceived as dominant have attempted to present themselves as an oppressed minority, such as white, middle-class heterosexual males. (C.f. Carolyn Louise Griffith's work.)

Chapter One

The Case for Higher Education

As an educator, when I think of the value of higher education, I think primarily about how people's lives are enriched by broadening their horizons, sharpening their critical thinking skills, increasing their appreciation for diversity, and deepening their understanding of our world. Higher education unquestionably offers a wealth of possibilities for transforming people's lives in positive ways.

However, many in our society want to measure higher education only in monetary terms: when they think about the value of higher education, they think in dollars and cents. And I suppose, given climbing tuitions and the state of our economy, it is understandable for people to try to assess what a degree is worth financially.

From the standpoint of monetary value, the latest figures comparing educational level, income, and employment couldn't be clearer. Higher levels of education consistently yield greater financial rewards. Individuals with higher levels of education are also more likely to be employed.

The average earnings of bachelor degree recipients working full-time in 2008 were $55,700 or $21,900 more than those of workers with high school diplomas alone. People with some college education but no degree earned 17% more than people with high school diplomas alone. For 20- to 24-year-old high school graduates, unemployment for the fourth quarter of 2009 for was a about two and a half times higher than for college graduates (Baum, Ma, and Payea 2010, 4).

Figure 1 (from *Education Pays 2010*) shows the expected lifetime earnings of people with various levels of education as compared with high school graduates. A quick glance at the data shows the greater earnings for people with some college but no degree, and then the marked increases at all levels of degree achievement, from associate's degrees to professional degrees. From the perspective of the strictly monetary payoff of a college education, the numbers are dramatically persuasive.

Baum, Ma, and Payea (2010) report that in our nation, the financial return associated with education beyond high school and the gaps in earnings by level of education have increased over time. These benefits of higher education are not only felt by individuals. Federal, state, and local governments profit from the increased tax revenues generated by college graduates. In addition, governments spend less on social support programs as citizens' incomes rise.

Other benefits of a college education include a greater likelihood of job satisfaction, health insurance, and pension benefits; a more active citizenry with healthier lifestyles; and increased parental involvement in educational activities with children, which leads to children being better prepared for school (Baum, Ma, and Payea 2010, 5).

The Profile of Today's College Students

Many of us may still picture the typical college student as someone who lives in dormitories, attends college full-time, and is aged 18-22. According to research by the Public Agenda (Johnson et al. 2009), that image is far off the mark:

- Forty-five percent of students in four-year institutions work more than 20 hours a week.
- Among those attending community colleges, 6 in 10 work more than 20 hours a week, and over a quarter work more than 35 hours a week.
- Just 25% of students attend the sort of residential college we often envision.
- A full 23% of college students have dependent children. (U.S. Department of Education 2010)

When educators say, "Today's college students are different from past generations," there is much truth to it. We often think of the differences in terms of fluency with technology and classroom behavior, but perhaps

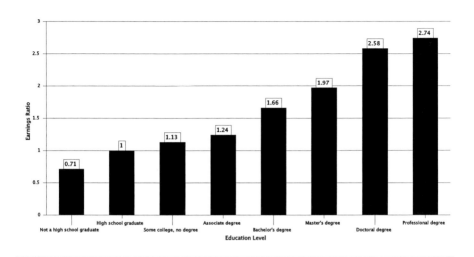

Figure 1: Expected Lifetime Earnings Relative to High School Graduates, by Education Level (Baum, Ma, and Payea 2010, 12). Source: Education Pays 2010: The Benefits of Higher Education for Individuals and Society. Copyright © 2010 The College Board. Reproduced with permission.

even more dramatic are differences in lifestyle, including differences related to income levels.

Certainly, in my years of teaching in the community college sector, more of my students struggled with finances, work, and family responsibilities than the students my colleagues taught at selective four-year institutions. It seemed that my colleagues' biggest complaint was their students' sense of entitlement, whereas I was often in awe of my students as I listened to what they were juggling in addition to their schoolwork.

Sometimes I would get annoyed when students repeatedly showed up late or missed class altogether . . . but then I would ask them to explain their behavior. I have too many stories to recount them all, so I will put down only two.

One student came to class about ten minutes late every morning. I asked to speak with her privately and was about to suggest that she set her alarm clock ten minutes earlier so she could be on time. Before I got the words out of my mouth, she said, "I know I have been consistently late. I have to get my siblings off to school and take my mom to chemotherapy three times a week, the same days as our class meets."

Another student, who sat in a front-row seat in my 220-person lecture, always came to class on time but suddenly, in the middle of the semester, stopped taking notes and stopped looking engaged. I thought he might be clinically depressed, the change in his demeanor was so striking. I talked with him privately and discovered that his brother had been shot. He was grieving but still attending his classes.

Perhaps these stories clarify my motivation for writing this book. The lives of low-income, first-generation, and minority students are often quite a struggle. I've met so many who genuinely want to succeed academically and need the extra help we can provide.

The Current Status of Degree Completion

The picture of degree completion in the United States is not encouraging.

Many educators have attempted to explain the quantity of students who drop out of the higher education pipeline: rising tuition costs, poor academic preparation / study skills, minimal student support and poor advisory services in high school and college, too many young people starting college without the motivation to see it through, and too many professors and advisers believing completion is solely the responsibility of students (Bowen, Chingos, and McPherson 2009).

A survey done by Public Agenda (Johnson et al. 2009) reports that the number one reason students give for leaving college is that they had to go to work and attend school at the same time and the stress was too much for them. More than half the students who left school offered this explanation. Little wonder, then, that students from low-income backgrounds fare so poorly in completing degrees.

Lumina Foundation for Education, a private entity that strives to help people achieve their potential by expanding access to and success in postsecondary education, released a report entitled, *A Stronger Nation through Higher Education: How and Why Americans Must Meet a 'Big Goal' for College Attainment* (2009). It makes the case for the urgency of getting more students into college and ensuring their success once they are there:

> Our nation—and every state within our nation—faces huge social and economic challenges. At Lumina Foundation for Education, we are convinced these challenges can be addressed only by educating many more people beyond high school. This means that we as a nation must continue to focus on approaches that make higher education more accessible and affordable for all. It

also means that all students who come to college must leave with meaningful, high-quality degrees and credentials so they can contribute to the workforce and provide for themselves and their families. Current economic conditions have only made this priority clearer and more urgent. (2009, 1)

The report goes on to state that "improving higher education success rates is a critical national priority, particularly in community colleges, where most low-income, first-generation students begin higher education" (Lumina Foundation for Education 2009, 5).

Since 2000, there have been a series of national and state report cards showing that America has fallen from top place in degree completion to someplace near the middle of the pack, internationally.

The National Center for Public Policy and Higher Education released a report (NCPPHE 2008a) entitled, *Measuring Up 2008: The National Report Card on Higher Education: Modest Improvements, Persistent Disparities, Eroding Global Competitiveness*. As one might glean from the title, this report indicates that college completion rates are substandard and have improved only slightly since 2000.

The Global Education Digest (UNESCO Institute for Statistics 2009) reports that in the United States, 40% of Americans hold an A.A. degree or higher, an attainment rate that has been about the same for the last forty years. The Organization for Economic Co-operation and Development (OECD), an international organization of the 30 most economically advanced countries, put the rate at 39% in 2008. This places America in the 12th position among 36 developed countries. America was number 1 in the world for postsecondary attainment for adults ages 25 to 34 for most of the post World War II period. This is obviously no longer the case.

World rankings from the OECD are illustrated in Figure 2. It shows degree completion rates for both the A.A. and the B.A. or equivalent in the age group of 25 to 34 year-olds. You'll easily find the United States. We are right behind other world leaders: the Russian Federation, Canada, Japan, Korea, Israel, New Zealand, Ireland, Belgium, Norway, France, and Denmark. After these, America follows. We can do better than this.

The latest report from *Education at a Glance* (Organization for Economic Co-operation and Development 2010) shows an international comparison of the population that has completed tertiary education (two- and four-year higher education programs) as of 2008 for two age groups: 25 to 24 year-olds and 55 to 64 year-olds. Figure 3 shows that in all countries except our own, younger people are far ahead of older population groups in

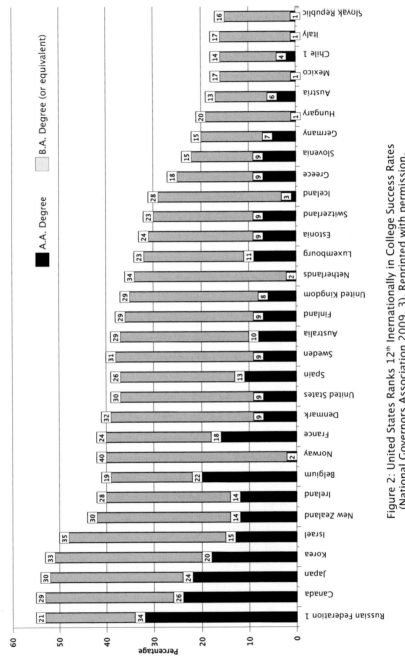

Figure 2: United States Ranks 12th Inernationally in College Success Rates (National Governors Association 2009, 3). Reprinted with permission.

educational attainment. Young people will be the world's future work force. Slipping behind in educating our youth puts America behind the global economic eight ball. (See Figure 3.)

The Lumina Report states that in some countries, more than 50% of young adults (25 to 34 years of age) are degree holders (Lumina Foundation for Education 2009). And the degree attainment rates in other countries continue to climb while America's rates remain flat. The Lumina Foundation estimates that at current college graduate production rates, there will be a shortage of 16 million college-educated adults in the American workforce by 2025.

Much past research has focused on the problem of access to college in the United States. However, the numbers indicate that a bigger problem is attrition. Low college-completion rates are partly attributable to the attrition rates for low-income, first-generation, historically underrepresented populations in higher education (Bowen, Chingos, and McPhearson 2009).

Over 40% of college students who earn more than ten college credits never complete a two or four-year degree, giving our nation the dubious distinction of being number one among "first world" nations whose younger people (18 to 24 years old) are *less* well educated than their older adults (25 and 65 years old). Americans 35 and older still rank among world leaders in terms of the proportion of them who are college educated; this reflects the educational progress of earlier times. Basically, we are losing "educational capital" among our younger generation. (Lumina Foundation for Education 2009)

Figures 4 through 7 show America's slippage in college enrollment internationally and the differences in educational attainment between 35 to 64 year-olds and 25 to 34 year-olds.

Figure 4 shows how far America has slipped in terms of enrolling traditional college-age students (18-24 year-olds). As of 2008, we were in 7th place, at 34%. The world leader was Korea, at 53%.

Figure 5 shows the United States in terms of college completion rates: square in the middle, with a ranking of 15 among 30 countries.

Figure 6 shows the percentage of older adults (35 to 64 year-olds) who hold at least an associate's degree. Here we are number 2 in the world, with only Canada ahead of us.

Figure 7 shows us just how far America's young adults have slipped. We are in 10th place for 25 to 34 year-olds who have earned either an associate's degree or a bachelor's degree.

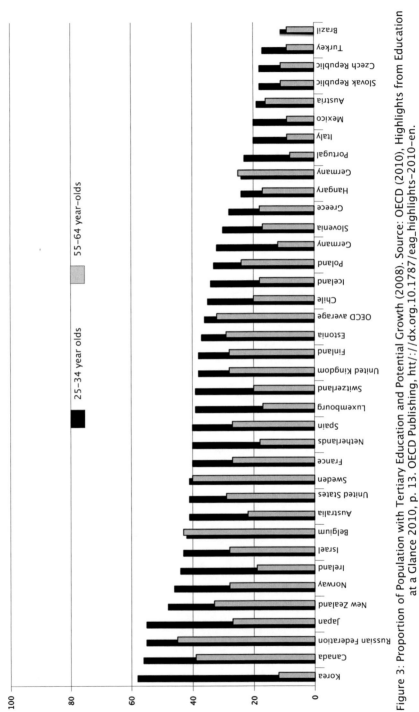

Figure 3: Proportion of Population with Tertiary Education and Potential Growth (2008). Source: OECD (2010), Highlights from Education at a Glance 2010, p. 13. OECD Publishing, htt/:://dx.org.10.1787/eag_highlights-2010-en.

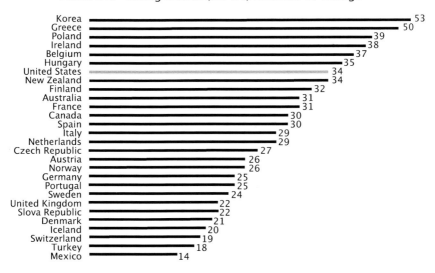

Figure 4. The U.S. Leadership in College Enrollment Has Slipped. (National Center for Public Policy and Higher Education 2008a, 6). Reprinted with permission.

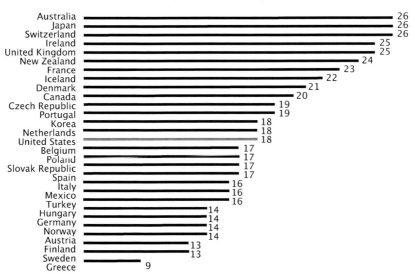

Figure 5: College Completion Has Never Been a U.S. Strength (National Center for Public Policy and Higher Education 2008a, 6). Reprinted with permission.

Percent of Adults (35–64 Holding an Associate's Degree or Higher

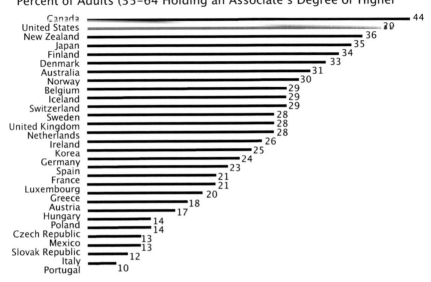

Figure 6: Educational Level of Older Americans Reflects Educational Progress of Earlier Times (National Center for Public Policy and Higher Education 2008a, 6). Reprinted with permission.

Percent of Adults (25–34) Holding an Associate's Degree or Higher

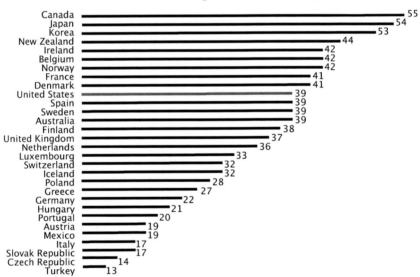

Figure 7: Educational Level (25–34) Holding an Associate's Degree or Higher (National Center for Public Policy and Higher Education 2008a, 6). Reprinted with permission.

The data show that the United States is faring pretty well internationally in bachelor's degree completion. The countries that are leaving us in the dust have done so by increasing attainment of associate's degrees. For example, Canada and Korea have almost 25% of their adults earning technical- and occupational-skill degrees, while only 9% of Americans do so.

The top six countries for degree holders are: Canada (55.8%), South Korea (55.5%), Russia (55.5%), Japan (53.7%), New Zealand (47.3%), and Ireland (43.9%).

Measuring Up (National Center for Public Policy and Higher Education 2008a) notes that compared to 2006, certain states of the U.S. did modestly better in preparing students to attend college; that is, more students were taking rigorous college preparation courses. (Some states showed more improvement than others. For example, Texas nearly tripled the number of high school students who had taken at least one upper-level science course.) However, the good news is overshadowed by the fact that even in this area, other nations are advancing more quickly than the United States. We continue to slip behind other countries in improving college opportunities for American high school students.

Additional significant findings from *Measuring Up* (National Center for Public Policy and Higher Education 2008a) are:

- While those who graduate from college are now more likely to have taken courses that prepared them for college (compared to the 1990s and the earlier part of this decade), far too many students graduate from high school underprepared to do college-level work and therefore need remediation. Moreover, a larger portion of students fail to graduate from high school than in the past, reducing the pool of potential college graduates and, thus, college-educated workers.

- Access to college is fairly flat in America, with small increases in some states and decreases in others.

- Dishearteningly, large disparities in higher-education performance persist in several dimensions—income, race/ethnicity, and geography— across states.

Further threatening America's place in the global workforce is the deterioration of college affordability. This is evidenced by two factors:

1. College tuition continues to outpace family income and the price of other living necessities; the former rises while the latter decreases or remains the same.

2. Students enrolling in college are taking on more debt to pay for it. More students are borrowing, and more students are borrowing more money than ever before. In the last 10 years, student borrowing has more than doubled.

In addition to slippage in college completion rates, data from OECD confirms America's slippage in college enrollment. Between 2003 and 2006, our nation fell from fifth to seventh place in the percentage of adults aged 18-24 enrolled in college. (For the same time period, the United States slipped from seventh to tenth place in the percentage of adults 25-34 holding an associate's degree or higher.)

Although America's rates of college enrollment have edged higher in recent years, decreases in affordability may curtail the rates for middle class families who have been relying on credit to send their children to college, and may put college entirely beyond the reach of low-income families.

There is general agreement these days that education and training beyond high school is necessary for the sort of employment that can sustain a middle-class life. The generation known as the "Baby Boomers" (1946 – 1964), the most highly educated group both currently and historically, is retiring or approaching retirement from the workforce. Baby Boomers must be replaced by younger workers.

In a recent report entitled *Help Wanted: Projections of Jobs and Education Requirements through 2018* (Carnevale, Smith, and Strohl 2010), researchers at Georgetown University's Center on Education and the Workforce predict *a significant shortfall of college graduates* to fill the job specifications that will be demanded in the coming decade. According to this report, by the year 2018, our nation will need 22 million new college degrees (associate's or higher) but will fall short by at least three million. The United States will also need at least 4.7 million new workers with postsecondary certificates.

Basically, the shortfall in educational attainment will translate into lost economic opportunity for millions of American workers and, by extension, lost economic opportunity for our nation. There will be a deficit of 300,000 college graduates annually between 2008 and 2018; this is largely because employers are demanding workers with high levels of education and training. To meet this demand, American colleges and universities would need to graduate 10% more students every year.

There are those who argue that our national budget deficit is too great to invest in education and that not everyone needs a college degree. For those people, and for all of us, the report *Help Wanted* sounds an alarm. As Jamie Merisotis, President and CEO of Lumina Foundation (which funded the *Help Wanted* research) has put it: "Instead of asking whether everyone needs to go to college, we should be asking if we can produce enough workers with high level degrees and credentials that meet the demands of the 21st century economy" (2010).

A College Degree — No Longer a Luxury

In today's economy, a college degree is no longer a luxury — it is a prerequisite for living a middle-class life. *Help Wanted* states that between 1973 and 2008, the percentage of jobs requiring higher education increased from 28% to 59%. The prediction for the future follows the same pattern. In the next ten years, the percentage of postsecondary graduate jobs will increase from 59% to 63%, leaving behind scores of high school graduates and dropouts. Higher education has become necessary for joining the middle and upper classes, rather than being just a preferred pathway. (2010)

Consider that in 1973, there were 25 million jobs available to people with some form of higher education. The number skyrocketed to 91 million in 2007. That's almost a four-fold increase in 34 years. Looking to the future, researchers see more of the same (Carnevale, Smith, and Strohl 2010).

Figure 8 shows education distribution across household income deciles and compares 1970 to 2017. The table reflects what many economists have been saying for quite some time: the middle class is shrinking and the gap between lower and upper income groups is getting wider.

But if the middle class is shrinking, then where are its members going? They seem to be dispersing in two opposite directions. Those without higher education are moving downward into the lower-income bracket, and those with higher education are moving upward into the higher-income bracket. If we are looking for one piece of data that is overwhelmingly persuasive about the monetary benefits of higher education, Figure 8 is it.

The *Help Wanted* report makes all this even clearer:

In the 37-year time frame shown in [Figure 8], the share of people with some college or Associate's degrees in the middle class declined from 53% to 45%. But the key to understanding this phenomenon is discerning where those people are going when they leave the middle. For example, the share of people with associate's degrees in the top three income deciles increased from around 28% to 35%. (2010)

1970	Lower-income Class (lower 3 deciles)	Middle-income Class (middle 4 deciles)	Upper-income Class (upper 3 deciles)
High school dropouts	39%	46%	15%
High school graduates	22%	60%	18%
Some college/ Associate's Degree	19%	53%	28%
Bachelor's Degree	16%	47%	37%
Graduate Degree	13%	46%	41%
2007			
High school dropouts	59%	33%	7%
High school graduates	35%	45%	19%
Some college	29%	45%	26%
Associate's Degree	20%	45%	35%
Bachelor's Degree	14%	38%	48%
Graduate Degree	9%	30%	61%

Figure 8: Education Distribution Across Household Income Deciles (1970/2007) (Carnevale, Smith, and Strohl 2010, 3). Reprinted with permission.

Therefore, while it is true that the middle class is declining, a more accurate portrayal of the American class dynamic would be to say that the middle class is dispersing into two opping streams of upwardly mobile college-haves and downwardly mobile college-have-nots.

Dropouts, high school graduates, and people with some college but no degree are on the down escalator of social mobility, falling out of the middle-income class and into the lower three deciles of family income. In 1970, almost half (46%) of high school drop-outs were in the middle class. By 2007, the share of dropouts in the middle class had fallen to 33%. In 1970, almost 60% of high school graduates were in the middle class. By 2007, the share had fallen to 45%.

Over that same period, people with college degrees (bachelor's and graduate degrees) have either stayed in the middle class or boarded the escalator upwards to the highest three family income deciles.

The share of people with bachelor's degrees in the middle class declined from 47% to 38%, decreasing by 9 percentage points. But the share of people with a bachelor's degree in the top three income deciles jumped from 37% to 48%. Meanwhile, the share of *people with graduate degrees* in the middle class declined from 46 to 30%—a decrease of 16 percentage points. But, *clearly, they were leaving [the middle class] for greener pastures,* as the share of people with graduate degrees in the top three income deciles increased from 41 to 61%. (Carnevale, Smith, and Strohl 2010, 3-4)

For those who are not yet convinced of the class distinctions in America and how higher education plays a role, consider Figure 9. It compares the earnings of high school dropouts, high school graduates, and people with some college or an A.A. degree with the earnings of college graduates. Notice how times have changed: from 1968 to the 1990s, bachelor's degree holders generally earned more money by a significant margin as compared to high school dropouts, high school graduates, and those with some college or an associate's degree. However, also notice the steepness of the curve since the 1990s in terms of bachelor's degree completers or better—the income gap has gotten considerably wider.

Figure 10, from *Help Wanted* (Carnevale, Smith, and Strohl 2010), shows the estimated average lifetime earnings differentiated by educational attainment. For the starkest contrast, compare the estimated average lifetime earnings of a high school graduate with those of someone who has earned a professional degree.

This data demonstrates a very strong positive correlation between educational attainment and socioeconomic status. Obviously, higher education pays off financially. Those with a college degree overwhelmingly do better than those without. Our society can indeed be seen as consisting of the degree "haves" and "have-nots." Here is where a vicious cycle begins: those who come from families in the have-not category, both in terms of

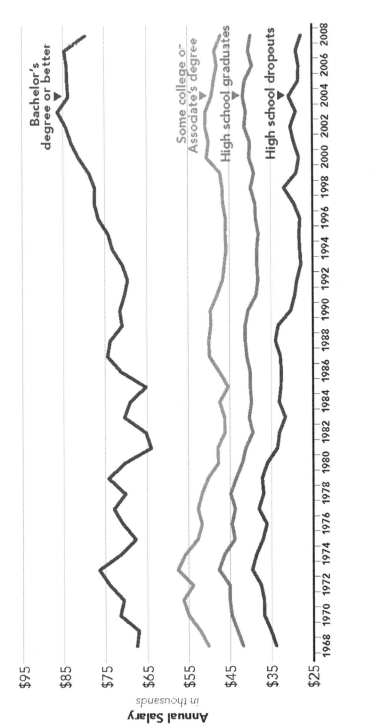

Figure 9: Wage Premium by Education (Carnevale, Smith, and Strohl 2010, 4). Reprinted with permission.

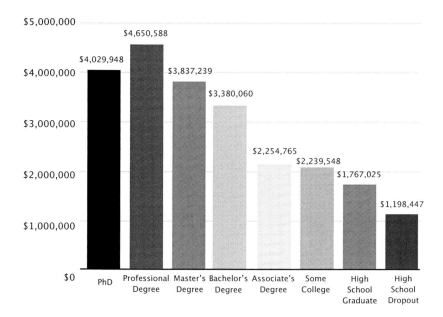

Figure 10: Estimated Average Lifetime Earnings by Education (in current dollars) (Carnevale, Smith, and Strohl 2010, 5). Reprinted with permission.

parents' income and educational level, have a much harder time gaining access to college and being successful once they are there. Perpetuation of class distinctions is an obvious outcome.

The Role of Income

Enrollment patterns and degree completion rates differ across income groups, and graduation rates differ according to type of institution attended. Baum, Ma, and Payea report that about 40% of students from families with incomes below $40,000 enrolled in public two-year colleges in the academic year 2007–2008, while 8% enrolled in for-profit institutions (2010). Only 17% of students from families earning $120,000 or higher enrolled in public two-year colleges, and only 1% attended for-profit institutions.

Figure 11 shows enrollment patterns of college students based on their families' income levels. Enrollment and completion in higher education are very different issues. While the income inequity between the haves and have-nots is clearly evident in enrollment patterns, there has neverthe-

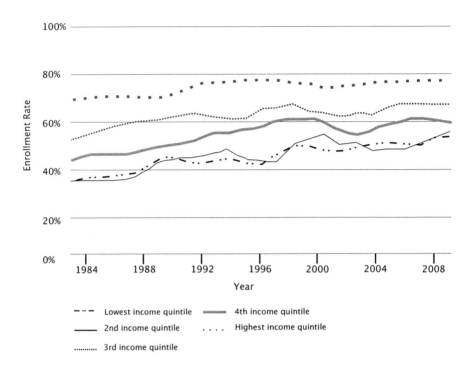

Figure 11: Postsecondary Enrollment Rates of Recent High School Graduates by Family Income (Baum, Ma, and Payea 2010, 35). Source: Education Pays 2010: The Benefits of Higher Education for Individuals and Society. Copyright © 2010 The College Board. Reproduced with permission.

less been a rise in *enrollments* among students from the lowest two quintiles. However, what we also need is higher *degree-completion* rates.

In terms of graduation-rate variations, Baum, Ma, and Payea found that for first-time, full-time students who began their studies for a bachelor's degree at a four-year college or university in 2002, 57% earned the degree within six years (2010). Completion rates averaged 65% at private not-for-profit institutions, 55% at public four-year colleges, and 22% at private for-profit institutions. The authors state,

> Students who attend the most selective colleges for which they are academically qualified are more likely to graduate than are similar students who "*undermatch*" by enrolling in colleges that do not match their qualifications…Students from lower-income backgrounds and those whose parents do not have college de-

grees are most likely to "undermatch," or enroll in less selective colleges than those for which they are qualified. (2010, 41)

Racial/Ethnic and Income Disparities Related to Preparation, Access, and Degree Completion Persist

Addressing the social value of higher education, Baum, Ma, and Payea state:

> Students who attend institutions of higher education obtain a wide range of personal, financial, and other lifelong benefits; likewise, taxpayers and society as a whole derive a multitude of direct and indirect benefits when citizens have access to post-secondary education. Accordingly, uneven rates of participation in higher education across different segments of U.S. society should be a matter of urgent concern not only to the individuals directly affected, but also to public policymakers at the federal, state, and local levels. (2010, 4)

Examining college enrollment by race/ethnicity from 1998 to 2004, we find that the gap separating the rates of White and Black high school graduates who enrolled in college within a year after high school was between 8% and 10%. By the year 2008, the gap between Black and White high school graduates enrolling in college grew to about 14%. In 2008, the college enrollment rate for White high school graduates was about 70%, while for Black high school graduates it was 56%. For Hispanic students, enrollment rates were 62% (Baum, Ma, and Payea 2010, 36). The gaps between White students and the underserved are widening rather than narrowing; this is obviously ominous news. Figure 12 gives a visual representation of this data.

Figure 13 shows the postsecondary enrollment rates of all high school graduates aged 18 to 24 by race/ethnicity for the years 1975-2008. In 2008, only 4.8% of Whites between the ages of 16 and 24 were not enrolled in high school or had not received a high school diploma. For the same period, the rate for Black students was 9.9% and for Hispanics it was 18.3%. As bleak as those numbers are, the situation is actually worse, since the numbers don't reflect military participation or incarceration. The enrollment gaps reported here exclude those two groups, with military participation and rates of incarceration being higher for Blacks and Hispanics.

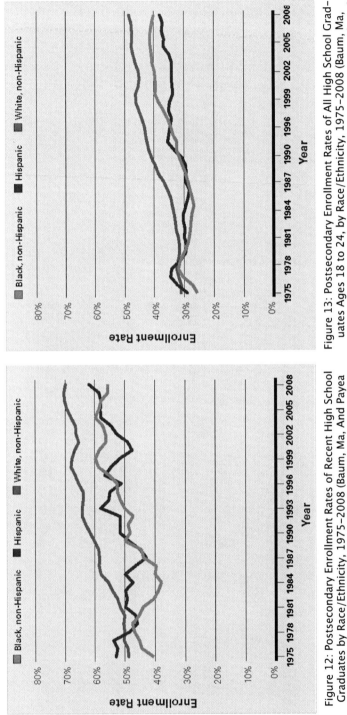

Figure 12: Postsecondary Enrollment Rates of Recent High School Graduates by Race/Ethnicity, 1975–2008 (Baum, Ma, And Payea 2010, 36). Source: Education Pays 2010: The Benefits of Higher Education for Individuals and Society. Copyright © 2010 The College Board. Reproduced with permission.

Figure 13: Postsecondary Enrollment Rates of All High School Graduates Ages 18 to 24, by Race/Ethnicity, 1975–2008 (Baum, Ma, And Payea 2010, 36). Source: Education Pays 2010: The Benefits of Higher Education for Individuals and Society. Copyright © 2010 The College Board. Reproduced with permission.

The level of education one achieves has a significant impact on one's lifetime earnings. Figure 14 illustrates that, once again, there are major disparities based on both race/ethnicity and gender.

Baum, Ma, and Payea also note the gender differences reflected in the latest graduation data:

> Among Blacks, Whites, and Hispanics, larger percentages of women than of men between the ages of 25 and 29 had bachelor's degrees in 2009. The gender gap was smallest for Blacks, among whom 21% of women and 18% of men in this age group had four-year college degrees. (2010, 49)

Additional findings noted in *Education Pays* are related to gender (Baum, Ma, Payea 2010, 49):

- In 1989, 26% of White men and 25% of White women between the ages of 25 and 29 had bachelor's degrees. Twenty years later, 32% of White men and 41% of White women in this age bracket had bachelor's degrees.
- About 10% of Hispanic men between the ages of 25 and 29 had bachelor's degrees in 2009, the same percentage as in 1989. The percentage with at least some college grew from 27% in 1989 to 30% in 2009.
- Among Black men between the ages of 25 and 29, the percentage with bachelor's degrees increased from 12% in 1989 and 13% in 1999 to 18% in 2009. The percentage of Black men with at least some college increased from 34% in 1989 to 45% in 1999, but remained at 45% a decade later.
- In 2009, 41% of White women, 21% of Black women, and 15% of Hispanic women between the ages of 25 and 29 had bachelor's degrees. The percentages with at least some college were 72%, 57%, and 41%, respectively.

Baum, Ma, and Payea make further distinctions between Hispanics' educational attainment in terms of native vs. foreign born, and country of origin:

> Educational attainment is higher for U.S.-born Hispanics than for Hispanic immigrants. Among adults 25 and older in 2008 and 2009, about 13% of those born outside the U.S. and 30% of those born in the U.S. to immigrant Hispanic mothers had some college experience but less than a bachelor's degree. About 20% of the second generation had at least a bachelor's degree, compared

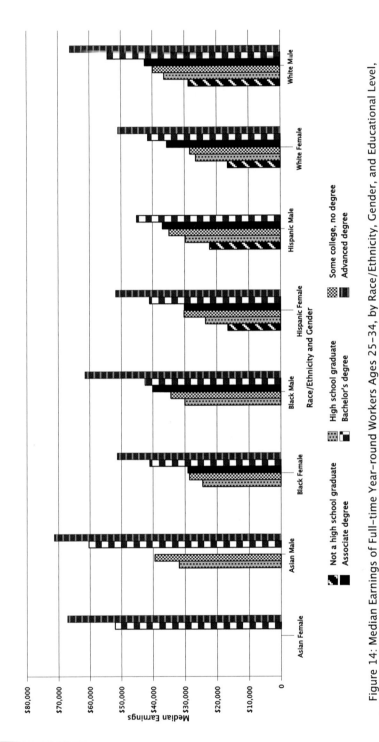

Figure 14: Median Earnings of Full-time Year-round Workers Ages 25–34, by Race/Ethnicity, Gender, and Educational Level, 2008 (Baum, Ma, and Payea 2010, 14). Source: Education Pays 2010: The Benefits of Higher Education for Individuals and Society. Copyright © 2010 The College Board. Reproduced with permission.

to only 11% of Hispanic immigrants… Hispanics include individuals from many different countries, with considerable variation in educational attainment rates. For example, both first and second-generation Mexican immigrants are much less likely than those from other Latin American countries to have completed college. (2010, 49)

Attainment

Thanks to demographic shifts in America, there are large, growing segments of young people poorly served by the higher education system. These younger generations are those whose educational opportunities and attainments reflect the systemic disadvantages associated with race/ethnicity, income, and geography.

According to The College Success Foundation's 10th Anniversary Report, *Unleashing America's Potential* (2010), only 10% of low-income, young American adults earn a bachelor's degree. Low-income students tend to enroll in less selective colleges with weak graduation rates (Roderick et al. 2008). About half a million low-income students who graduate in the top half of their high school graduating classes don't earn a degree within eight years of high school (Carnevale 2009).

As Lerner and Brand's research shows, all students (but especially low-income, first-generation students) need academic and social support to help them navigate the system towards a bachelor's degree (2006).

According to Engle and Tinto's *Moving Beyond Access: College Success for Low-Income, First-Generation Students*, low-income, first-generation students are more likely than their more advantaged peers to have the following characteristics:

> To be older, female, have a disability, come from minority backgrounds, to be non-native English speakers and to have been born outside the U.S., to have dependent children and to be single parents, to have earned a high school equivalency diploma, and to be financially independent from their parents. (2008, 8)

They claim that low-income, first-generation college students are also more likely to "delay entry into postsecondary education after high school, attend college closer to home, live off-campus, attend part-time, and work full-time while enrolled."

Demographic Risk Factors

Previous research shows that these demographic and social characteristics are risk factors for degree completion, especially for the completion of the B.A. Degree (Chen 2005; Choy 2000). The risk factors are often overlapping, as in enrolling part-time in college, working full-time, and parenting. In the academic year of 2003-2004, low-income, first-generation students had an average of three risk factors (Engle and Tinto 2008).

Low-income, historically underserved students face myriad challenges that interfere with their success in high school and in college: Financial barriers limit their choices. If they are admitted to college, and are the first in their families to attend college, they do not have the advantages of coming from a college-going family culture. Add to this an educational system that does not properly prepare them for college-level work, and the odds are strongly tilted against them.

Let's look at the data provided by the U.S. Department of Education on college graduation rates across the board, by race/ethnicity, and by gender (2010).

Across the board:

> Approximately 57% of first-time students seeking a bachelor's degree or its equivalent and attending a 4-year institution full time in 2001–02 completed a bachelor's degree or its equivalent at that institution in 6 years or less.

By race/ethnicity:

> Bachelor's degree completion rates of students seeking a bachelor's degree at 4-year institutions varied by student characteristics, including race/ethnicity and sex. Asian/Pacific Islander students had the highest 6-year graduation rate, followed by White, Hispanic, Black, and American Indian/Alaska Native students. Approximately 67% of Asians/Pacific Islanders, compared with 60% of Whites, 48% of Hispanics, 42% of Blacks, and 40% of American Indians/Alaska Natives graduated with a bachelor's degree or its equivalent within 6 years. This pattern held for Asians/Pacific Islanders, Whites, and Hispanics at each institution type while Blacks and American Indians/Alaska Natives consistently had the lowest graduation rates of the five racial/ethnic groups.

By gender:

> In both public and private not-for-profit 4-year institutions, the 6-year graduation rates for females were higher than the rates for males. For public institutions, approximately 58% of females seeking a bachelor's degree or its equivalent graduated within 6 years, compared with 52% of their male counterparts; for private not-for-profit institutions, 67% of females graduated within 6 years, compared with 61% of males. At private for-profit institutions, however, the 6-year graduation rate was higher for males than females (28 vs. 21%).

The achievement gaps between White students and African American and Hispanic students are evident in high school, with four-year diploma completion at 69.2% for Whites, 51.2% for African Americans, and 55% for Hispanics (Editorial Projects in Education 2009).

> The evidence is overwhelming that higher education improves people's lives, makes our economy more efficient, and contributes to a more equitable society. The existing gaps in participation and success are detrimental not only to individual lives, but also to society as a whole. Different paths are appropriate for different individuals, and our challenge is to make the most promising paths readily available to students from all backgrounds. We will all be better off if we continue to make progress in this direction. (Baum, Ma, Payea 2010, 9)

Income Disparities in Degree Completion

Family income disparities as they relate to completion are particularly striking: 23.1% of students in the lowest economic quartile earn a B.A. by age 24, as opposed to 95% of students in the top quartile (Mortenson 2009). In *Family Income and Educational Attainment 1970 to 2008*, Mortenson reports that:

> This analysis [data gathered by the Census Bureau through the Current Population Survey] highlights the stunning commitment of higher education to the education of children from affluent families, and the relative indifference to children born from families in the bottom half of the family income distribution. While this has been the historical tendency of higher education, these data show that this view [that the elite should be most

highly educated] has strengthened dramatically since the advent of the Regressive Policy Era around 1980. (2009, 14)

Colleges Can Promote Student Success for the Underserved

The Education Trust, established in 1990 by the American Association for Higher Education to encourage colleges and universities to support K-12 reform efforts, released two reports in August 2010: *Big Gaps, Small Gaps: Some Colleges and Universities Do Better Than Others in Graduating Hispanic Students* and *Big Gaps, Small Gaps: Some Colleges and Universities Do Better Than Others in Graduating African American Students.* Both reports paint a fairly comprehensive picture of which colleges/universities are succeeding in narrowing the racial/ethnic gaps and which colleges/universities have a long way to go.

The goal of The Education Trust is to close the gaps in opportunity and achievement that prevent far too many young people—especially those from low-income families and those who are Black, Latino, or American Indian, from living their lives on the margins of the American mainstream.

The basic tenets of the Education Trust are:

1. Students will learn at high levels when there are high expectations for their learning.

2. Closing the achievement gaps that separate low-income students and students of color from other students is central to our nation's future.

Both reports go beyond looking at national college-graduation averages. Instead, they examine disaggregated six-year graduation rates at hundreds of America's public and private colleges and universities. At nearly two thirds of the colleges and universities in the study, fewer than half the African American students earn a degree. Over 60% of the public colleges and universities attended by the vast majority of Hispanic students graduated less than 50% of those students in 6 years.

Teasing out racial/ethnic disparities, the *Big Gaps/Small Gaps* reports found that for underrepresented minorities, the college success rate was lower (24%), while for other students it was higher (38%). In fact, only 7% of minority students who entered community colleges earned bachelor's degrees within a ten year period.

What both reports make clear is that the large gaps in completion rates between White students and African American and Hispanic students are not inevitable. Institutions with similar student body makeups and similarities across other crucial dimensions vary in their student success rates. Obviously this means some colleges and universities have instituted policies and practices that prove successful in narrowing achievement gaps. Chapter 3 explores "best practices" of the colleges and universities with the smallest racial/ethnic gaps in degree completion.

Also from the Education Trust, Engle and Theokas (2010) report in *Top Gap Closers* that the key ingredient necessary for closing achievement gaps is for institutions to focus on student success and make closing achievement gaps a top priority. Those public colleges and universities that were most successful either narrowed or completely closed the gaps between underserved minority students—African Americans, Hispanics, and American Indians—and their White and Asian peers.

Promoting
Hispanic Student Success

Given the demographic shifts in our population, educating Hispanic students is critical to our standing in the world, not only in terms of degree-completion rates, but also in terms of the global economy. Latino students will compose about 25% of the nation's college-aged population by the year 2025. Increasing the number of college graduates overall must focus on improving Hispanic students' degree-completion rates or the nation's goals will never be met.

To get a sense of the major demographic shifts in our population, see the changes in percentages and share of total change for the time span 2000 to 2008 in Figure 15 (from the PEW Hispanic Center). Notice that native and foreign-born Hispanics account for 51.3% of the share of total change across racial/ethnic groups.

The organization *Excelencia in Education* aims to accelerate higher education success for Latino students by providing data-driven analysis of the educational status of Latino students and by promoting education policies and institutional practices that support their academic achievement. Their recent report, *The Condition of Latinos in Education: Factbook 2008* (compiled by Deborah Santiago, Vice President for policy and research at *Excelencia*), synthesizes national and public data into a series of one-page fact sheets. These provide snapshots of the progress of Latinos in education,

	2008 population	2000 population	Change, 2000–2008	Percent change, 2000–2008	Share of total change (%)
Hispanic	46,822,476	35,204,480	11,617,996	33.0	51.3
• Native born	28,985,169	21,072,230	7,912,939	37.6	35.0
• Foreign born	17,837,307	14,132,250	3,705,057	26.2	16.4
White alone, not Hispanic	198,963,659	194,527,123	4,436,536	2.3	19.6
Black alone, not Hispanic	36,774,337	33,706,554	3,067,783	9.1	13.6
Asian alone, not Hispanic	13,227,070	10,088,521	3,138,549	31.1	13.9
Other, not Hispanic	8,272,186	7,895,228	376,958	4.8	1.7

Figure 15: Population Change by Race and Ethnicity: 2000 and 2008 (PEW Hispanic Center 2008). Reprinted with permission.
http//pewhispanic.org/factsheets/factsheet.php??factsheetID=58.

and clearly show the strengths and weaknesses for Hispanic students throughout the educational pipeline.

The Condition of Latinos in Education: Factbook 2008 reports that in 2006, Hispanic students represented 12% of undergraduates. In 2006-2007, Hispanics represented 13% of undergraduates. Hispanics have lower levels of educational attainment than any other group in America. In 2007, only 13% of Hispanics aged 25 and over had earned a bachelor's degree or higher, compared with 32% of Whites and 19% of Blacks.

In addition, during the academic year of 2005-2006, Hispanics earned 11% of all associate's degrees and just 7% of bachelor's degrees from degree-granting institutions. Planty et al. (2009) found that in 2008, Latinos earned only 12% of associate's degrees and 8% of bachelor's degrees.

The modest strides Hispanics have made in earning degrees over the last decade are tempered by the fact that they are not improving as quickly as other groups. Looking at the period 1975 to 2007, the percentage of Hispanics with a B.A. or higher degree nearly doubled: from 7% to 13%. However, in that same time period, the percentage of Whites with a bachelor's degree or higher *more* than doubled: from 15% to 32%. And for Blacks in America, the number of degree holders tripled: from 6% to 19%.

Latino success is absolutely necessary in order to improve our nation's degree-completion rates and workforce readiness for three reasons: the projected population growth of Latinos, their current poor educational attainment levels, and their relative youth.

Latino population demographics suggest difficult challenges to college access and successful participation. For example, Latino students are more likely to be the first in their families to attend college, more likely than other undergraduates to be enrolled part-time, and more likely than other undergraduates to come from low-income families.

A report entitled *Taking Stock: Higher Education and Latinos* (Santiago and Reindl 2009), compiled for *Excelencia in Education,* shows percentages of young people 18 to 24 years old who earned associate's degrees or higher. Asians in America made up 25% of the A.A. and B.A. degree holders among this younger population. Whites made up 15%, while Hispanics made up 8% and Blacks made up 9%. Among the population 25 and older, Asians make up 59% of degree holders, while Whites account for 39%, Hispanics 19% and Blacks 29%. The data show that whether looking at young adults or adults aged 25 and older, in 2008, Latinos earned fewer degrees than all other groups.

Two recent reports published by the PEW Hispanic Center, Mark Hugo Lopez's *Latinos and Education: Explaining the Attainment Gap* (2009) and Richard Fry's *The Changing Pathways of Hispanic Youths into Adulthood* (2009), show that *although Hispanic youths place a great value on higher education, with 90% of Hispanic youths saying that a college degree is important for success in life, only about half say they plan to get a degree themselves.*

Hispanics place an even greater value on higher education than the overall population does: 88% percent of Hispanics agree that a college degree is important for success in life, as opposed to 74% of the general public.

Then why is there an apparent contradiction between Hispanics' values and aspirations and their actual achievement? The survey data from this pair of reports clearly explains the contradiction in economic terms — the biggest reason Hispanic youths drop out of the educational pipeline to a college degree is *financial pressure to help support a family.* Of 16- to

25-year-old Hispanic survey respondents, 74% halted their education either prior to or right after high school graduation in order to support their families. To this we might add the 40% of Hispanics who say they cannot afford to go to school, with or without a family to support. Obviously, financial barriers are a prominent explanation for the educational achievement gap between Hispanics and Whites.

State by State Analysis
of Degree Completion

One Lumina Report, *A Stronger Nation through Higher Education* (2009), did a state by state analysis of degree completion based on Census data beginning in the year 2000. This data is part of the global degree-attainment data from the OECD which focuses on monitoring and analyzing economic trends. Each fall, OECD releases an updated report, *Education at a Glance*, that offers data on a range of education indicators.

Figure 16 shows the quantity of people per country who receive B.A. degrees by the typical age. Once again, the United States lags behind, with only 35.5% of its general population completing a bachelor's degree by the typical graduation age. Compare this with Iceland's 62.8%, Australia's 59.6%, Finland's 57.3%, and New Zealand's 53.5%.

All the data points to the same conclusion: the United States is falling behind many other countries in educational attainment.

International Differences in Degree Completion

The reasons for the difference in postsecondary achievement rates between our nation and others may reflect demographic shifts, declining numbers of young people in some countries, differences in levels of immigration, and probably other factors as well. That said, it is clear that some countries, such as Ireland, the U.K. and Korea, are making concerted efforts to raise levels of postsecondary education though policies such as expanding capacity and lowering costs.

Many Americans mistakenly assume that our nation can remain competitive in a global economy by educating a small, elite group that will drive innovation. Contrary to this view, the advanced economies of Europe, Asia, and Oceania operate on the assumption that overall level of educational attainment is a truer measure of the vitality of an economy. There is substantial empirical data supporting this premise.

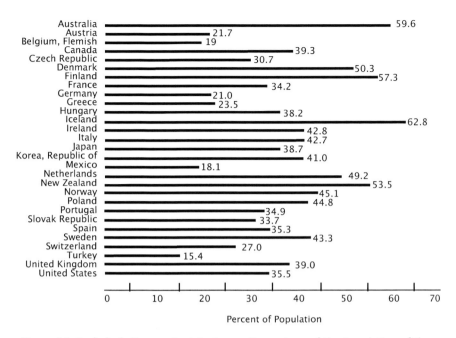

Figure 16: Bachelor's Degree Recipients as a Percentage of the Population of the Typical Ages of Graduation, by Country: 2006 (National Center for Education Statistics 2009). Reprinted with permission from UNESCO Institute for Statistics, uis.

Economic Demands and Educational Levels

The clearest evidence supporting the view that overall level of educational attainment reflects real economic demands can be seen in the growing gap in earnings based on education level. In 29 of the 30 OECD member countries, the wage gap is widening between people who have completed some postsecondary education and those who have not. This is despite the fact that the proportion of college graduates in the workforce is increasing.

If the economy were not demanding higher levels of knowledge and skills, the earnings gap could be expected to narrow. In other words, in a world of supply and demand, the earnings gap would narrow as the supply of college graduates increased. This is not so globally or in the United States.

In the United States since 1975, the average earnings of high school dropouts have fallen 15%, and the average earnings of high school graduates have fallen by 1%. On the other hand, the earnings of college graduates for the same period have risen by 19%. The economic benefits of

41

higher education, both for individuals and for the economy as a whole, are irrefutable.

The gap in educational attainment contributes to the disparities in income among racial/ethnic groups in the United States, and as the population of historically underserved groups expands, the earnings gap will become even larger.

Looking back at Figure 10 from *Help Wanted* (Carnevale, Smith, Strohl 2010, 5), we see that it estimates lifetime earnings by educational level. The chart shows that:

- A high school degree is worth about $569,000 more than being a dropout.
- Having some college but no degree or a postsecondary certificate is worth about $473,000 more than a high school degree.
- An associate's degree is worth about $15,000 more than some college but no degree.
- A bachelor's degree is worth about $1.1 million more than an associate's degree.
- A master's degree is worth $457,000 more than a bachelor's degree.

To see a visual representation of the annual median earnings of people at various levels of education, see Figure 17. It depicts the annual median earnings and educational attainment of persons 25 years old and over who are full-time wage and salary workers. The data could not be clearer—the more education one has, the higher the salary one earns. Notice in particular that a high school graduate earns an average of $30,732 while a person with a doctorate or professional degree earns about $80,000 (based on 2008 dollars).

Clearly, those voices proclaiming that higher education is no longer necessary or lucrative are not reading the latest findings.

Compounding the problem, too many people ignore or deny the ramifications of America's changing demographics.

A Stronger Nation through Higher Education (Lumina Foundation for Education 2009, 3) states:

Of the predicted U.S. population growth of 56 million between 2000 and 2020, 46 million will be members of minority groups. The U.S. is projected to become a "majority minority" country by 2050.

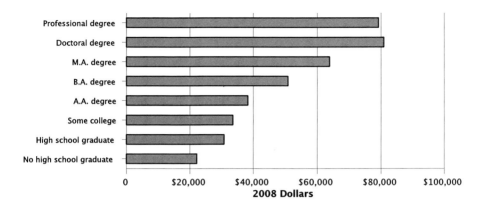

Figure 17: Annual Median Earnings and Educational Attainment (National Governors Association 2009, 2). Reprinted with permission.

This report emphasizes what many studies have previously shown: the rates of college attainment for America's underserved students (i.e., first-generation college students, low-income students, and students of color) are significantly lower than college attainment rates of other groups of students.

Education success gaps, which have been with us for decades, are widening. While the percentage of White, non-Hispanic American adults having at least four years of college (30%) is not commendable when compared with other nations, only 18% of African Americans and 12% of Hispanics have achieved that level of education. Given the current demographic and economic trends in the United States, this widening gap is an ominous sign.

When students drop out of the higher education system, they lose, their states lose, and the nation loses, all in terms of economic potential.

Unemployment is greatly impacted by level of education and race/ethnicity. Figure 18 shows that unemployment decreases markedly as the level of education achieved increases for all groups.

Our nation must make significant headway in increasing educational access, affordability, and college completion rates if America is to regain its footing on the global educational and economic stage. As Baum, Ma, and Payea state (2010, 8):

Solid evidence indicates that our main focus should be providing opportunities for postsecondary preparation and access, and supporting more students in making choices that will allow them to maximize their postsecondary education success.

Chapter 2 shows how faculty in postsecondary education can work towards helping more students achieve academic success.

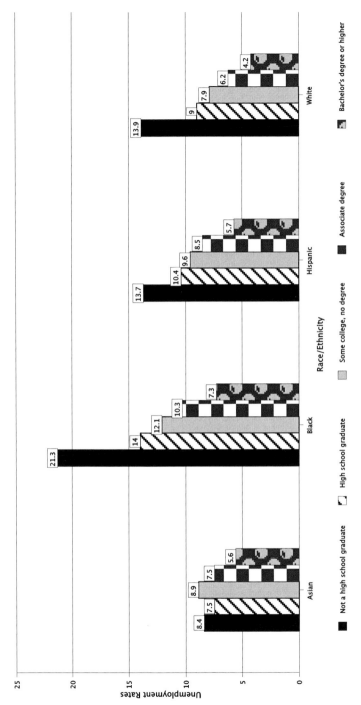

Figure 18: Unemployment Rates of Individuals Ages 25 and Older, by Education Level and Race/Ethnicity, 2009 (Baum, Ma, and Payea 2010, 21). Source: Education Pays 2010: The Benefits of Higher Education for Individuals and Society. Copyright © 2010 The College Board. Reproduced with permission.

Improving Graduation Rates through Effective Teaching

I have heard many faculty members over the years put the onus of learning and academic success squarely on the shoulders of their students. They say, "Not everyone belongs in college. How can I teach an underprepared student or a student who lacks motivation?" I understand their perspective, but I don't share it.

There is certainly truth to the notion that many students are underprepared to be successful in college. However, given the current situation, in which a certificate or degree is a prerequisite to a middle class life and necessary for our nation to stay competitive economically, we cannot justify nor afford leaving some people behind. Being underprepared for college-level work should not exclude people from higher education. The challenge is for us to prepare students to be able to achieve. As Kuh et al. (2005, 78) so elegantly put it, "teach the students you have, not the students you wish you had."

Lack of motivation is, for some students, a barrier to learning and success. And I agree with those faculty members who say, "We cannot *give* motivation to a student who lacks it." Yes, but as teachers, we can inspire students and help them to develop motivation. We can't give motivation to them on a silver platter, but we can make a difference in whether or not we spark their interest and curiosity, and thus their motivation to learn.

What I describe in this chapter are aspects of the learning environment and proven pedagogical strategies that help *all* students to learn.

While all students benefit from inclusive, welcoming, learner-centered classrooms that use active learning strategies, research shows that first generation, low-income, and minority students reap the greatest benefit.

It is widely accepted among educators that pedagogical techniques aimed at "engaging" students—involving them deeply in the material they study and in the process of learning—promote success. Research (e.g., the National Survey of Student Engagement [NSSE] and the version specifically for community colleges, Community College Survey of Student Engagement [CCSSE]) has qualitatively and quantitatively supported this belief.

Two recent studies have found strong evidence that engagement strategies work for underserved and underprepared students in particular. Both studies were done by powerhouses in the learning assessment world. George D. Kuh, Chancellor's Professor and director of the Center for Postsecondary Research at Indiana University, led both studies. The first study, "Connecting the Dots: Multi-Faceted Analyses of the Relationships between Student Engagement Results from the NSSE," examined the academic performance of about 11,000 freshman and seniors at 18 four-year institutions that used NSSE to measure how engaged their students are in the learning process.

Kuh's et al. (2007) second study matched colleges' NSSE results with (1) other data about students' academic preparation and demographic background, and (2) their first-year college grades and their persistence to the sophomore year.

The research results of Kuh and his colleagues (2007; 2008) clearly reflect the benefits of engagement practices for the underserved and underprepared. In fact, not only do engagement practices work for the academically underprepared and minority population, but these pedagogical techniques seem to make a *bigger* difference for these students than for students in general.

A compelling finding of "Connecting the Dots"(Kuh et al. 2007) is that as Hispanic students became more academically engaged, their academic performance improved more sharply than that of their white peers. Moreover, at higher levels of engagement, Hispanic students outperformed their white cohort. There were similar findings for African American students. At the highest levels of academic engagement, African American students were more likely to return to college for the sophomore year than were similarly engaged white students.

At long last we have persuasive evidence of the benefits of active engagement techniques, not only for all students, but specifically for historically underserved students, who will make up more and more of America's student body.

The most significant place in which we begin to facilitate the motivation of our students—*all* our students—to learn and to do well is in the first day of class, when we first meet them.

Classroom Atmosphere, College Culture, and Retention

> I've learned that people will forget what you said. People will forget what you did, but people will never forget how you made them feel. —Maya Angelou

When I was in college many years ago, I remember quite a few of my professors starting the semester by telling us how difficult their courses were and how many students failed to pass them. I also remember one particular moment of my student orientation: the Dean of the college told us to look at the person to the left and the person to the right, and then he said, "Only one of the three of you will earn a degree."

Is this the kind of classroom environment or college culture that inspires and excites students to start their journeys of discovery in higher education? Not so much, I think. And on a related note, if what the Dean said were true, is a 33 % graduation rate something of which a college should be proud? Is this orientation approach considered to be motivational?

Psychologists tell us that there are two kinds of motivation: *intrinsic motivation*, motivation from within ourselves, and *extrinsic motivation*, which is external to us. Intrinsic motivation in the college context has to do with wanting to learn because we are naturally intellectually curious, and we desire to know more. Extrinsic motivation has to do with wanting to learn in order to get some external reward, such as an "A" on an exam or the ultimate goal of a college degree.

Students are often lured by external rewards. This is quite probably a function of a history of conditioning, often from their families, and certainly from the school system. One of the questions that often irritates college professors is when students ask, "Will this be on the test?" We are disheartened because we perceive the questioner to be only extrinsically motivated, and wish for something more intrinsic. Often that question has more to do with the pressure that students feel to do well—not that they are exclusively grade-oriented.

Although students can plod through to a college degree with only extrinsic motivation, intrinsic motivation is what will ultimately be more fulfilling to the student and will yield a greater benefit for society as a whole. Intellectually curious students have a better chance of developing the critical thinking skills that are becoming more essential in a complex world, a world that requires high-level problem solvers.

Inspiring students to develop intrinsic motivation is part and parcel of the kind of classroom atmosphere we need to create. Cognitive psychologists tell us that whether or not a student *learns* (cognitive domain) cannot be separated from how the student *feels* (affective domain). Wilkinson and Ansell say it best:

> The emotional climate of the classroom is directly related to the attainment of academic excellence, however defined. Students' feelings about what they experience in class — whether inclusion or exclusion, mastery or inadequacy, support or hostility — cannot be divorced from what and how well they learn. (1992, 4)

Retention literature describes factors that lead to student persistence and has a wealth of data supporting the role of the affective dimension. In fact, research shows that one of the most important factors in whether students will complete a degree at a particular institution is whether or not they have friends at the same college. Do they have a *sense of belonging* within the campus community?

As an educator, I am concerned about how students *feel* in class because how they feel in class (and how they feel at their particular institution as a whole) has a profound effect on whether or not they succeed.

Where will our students develop a sense of community at our colleges and universities? At commuter schools and community colleges, where students often come to class and then rush off to work or to meet family responsibilities, probably the only place where that can happen is in our classrooms. Chances are that even at residential colleges, for students who do not become actively engaged with the institution through sports, clubs, or college governance, the classroom is the only opportunity for community building.

In order to promote student success and academic persistence to a degree, we need to create a welcoming and inclusive classroom atmosphere where students from diverse backgrounds feel safe. Students need to feel that their voices will be heard and that their opinions are valued by educators and by their classmates. Within an atmosphere of safety and respect, the seeds of friendship formation are planted. Cultivating an atmosphere of trust and warmth between the teacher and the students, and among the students in the class, begins the first time they all meet.

The First Day(s) of the Semester

The first day of class is the point at which classroom atmosphere starts taking shape; in the end, the teacher is responsible for creating an environment conducive to learning. Just as the teacher should ensure physical safety and comfort, he or she should ensure that all students feel welcome.

As mentioned, the bottom line for whether or not a student stays at a college or university probably has more to do with personal connections than with studies. This may be truer now than ever before, as we witness the millennial generation (those students born between 1982 and 2002) connecting socially through cell phones, texting, and Facebook, unlike any previous generation.

If social connections are going to happen in our classrooms, the first day(s) of the semester are critical for setting the proper tone for community building. The first day of class should result in students wanting to come to the next class. How can this be accomplished? In that first day, use an icebreaker.

There are many icebreakers to choose from and they all have one thing in common: after the icebreaker, students feel more at ease. Sometimes icebreakers use humor; mostly, they get students to interact with one another.

The most important goals for that first day and the few classes immediately following are:

- teachers begin to learn students' names,
- students meet at least a few other students,
- teachers introduce themselves in a way that makes them seem approachable,
- teachers clearly describe their expectations for their course and tell students what they need to do in order to be successful.

First-generation Students

We can no longer assume that students know what it actually means to be a college student, especially those students who are the first in their families to go to college. Even the experience of navigating the college admissions process involves a marked contrast between students from middle-class families with college-educated parents and students whose parents don't have a clue as to what it is all about.

Navigating the admissions process, including financial aid applications, can be a daunting experience even for college-educated parents. It's an absolute quagmire for the rest of the populace. Many of the students looking at us expectantly that first day may be riddled with anxiety and confusion. How do we put them at ease, encourage them, help them assimilate to college, and guide them to be successful in our classes? I find it helps to remind myself of times I've attempted something brand new and the accompanying anxiety I felt. Educators can no longer think of themselves as simple conveyors of the knowledge of a discipline. Not only is that out of fashion among educators, it probably made little sense when it was in fashion.

Now we must see ourselves as knowledge experts, yes, but also as much more. We are mentors, advisors, sometimes personal counselors, guides, coaches, and facilitators. A good teacher is student-oriented much more than content-oriented.

Lest I lose anyone with that last statement, let me say that I know what a challenge it is to wear so many hats. I taught at a community college for thirty-five years. I also want to allay fears that because I claim good teachers are more student-centered than content-centered, I am not concerned with high academic standards. I am concerned.

My philosophy is not about "touchy-feely" classroom activity solely designed to make people feel good. My philosophy is grounded in a review of the educational literature on maintaining high academic standards *and* increasing retention and degree completion. These are not mutually exclusive goals. In fact, setting high expectations for students actually increases retention rates.

The Case for Active Learning

Human beings are most likely to learn deeply when they are trying to solve problems or answer questions that they have come to regard as important, intriguing, or beautiful. —Ken Bain and James Zimmerman, *Understanding Great Teaching* (2009)

In Chickering and Gamson's *Seven Principles for Good Practice*, they note:

Learning is not a spectator sport. Students do not learn much just by sitting in class listening to teachers, memorizing prepackaged assignments, and spitting out answers. They must talk about what they are learning, write about it, relate it to past experiences, apply it to their daily lives. They must make what they learn part of themselves. (1987, 3-7)

Bonwell and Eison state that active learning involves five common factors (1991). These are:

1. student involvement beyond mere listening;

2. more emphasis on the development of skills and less on transmittal of information;

3. student involvement in higher order thinking skills;

4. student involvement in activities, such as reading, discussing, and writing; and

5. emphasis on students' exploration of values and attitudes.

Although interest in active learning is high and research supporting its efficacy abounds, a great number of teaching faculty still rely primarily on the lecture technique. After all, that is how most of us, particularly my own (Baby Boomer) generation, were taught. Many lecturers have some misunderstanding about what active learning means and feel a bit threatened that the active learning movement is suggesting they no longer lecture. They fear that they will lose precious class time to "activities" and won't be able to cover all their material.

Mini-Lectures and Interactive Lectures

The use of active learning strategies does not negate or replace the lecture mode. That would be a little like throwing the baby out with the bath water. Instead, lectures can become "mini lectures"of about 15 to 20 minutes, which corresponds to the average adult attention span (Penner 1984). They can be followed by very brief activities and exercises that can help students to better learn and retain what they have heard.

I am also suggesting that even mini-lectures ought to be interactive. The traditional mode of lecturing to an audience may work for some students, perhaps the more mature adult. However, students of the millennial generation and those who are tired and unmotivated will not stay tuned in and will certainly not develop higher-order critical thinking skills by simply listening.

Die-hard lecturers, facing students with glazed eyes, have often tried to make their lectures more dazzling, more entertaining, and more engaging. Indeed, we *can* become more dynamic lecturers and there are guides to help us. Silberman offers suggestions for getting students' attention at the beginning of a lecture and then maintaining it during the presentation itself. Among Silberman's suggestions are (1996, 19-21):

- Start your lecture with an interesting story or anecdote that grabs students' attention.
- Begin the lecture with a provocative visual, such as a cartoon.
- Pose a problem or ask a question that is at the center of the lecture so that students will be motivated to stay tuned in.
- Limit the major points of your lecture. Present key terms and concepts on an overhead transparency or whiteboard to help students remember them. (Update: PowerPoint slides)
- Use plenty of real-life examples and comparisons, and try to relate your information to your students' previous experiences.
- Wherever possible, use transparencies, flip charts, and handouts to give your students a visual as well as an auditory channel of learning. (Update: PowerPoint, Video, Internet)
- Periodically, stop lecturing so that you can ask students to give examples of the concepts you've presented so far.
- Present a problem or question for students to address based on the information covered in the lecture.
- Toward the end of the lecture, give students a test or quiz on the topic covered. [Note: I don't use this particular technique myself, for fear that students will anxiously focus on details instead of listening to the big picture of the topic. However, colleagues who use the technique have had success with it. They tell students ahead of time that there will be a short quiz at the end of class that asks them to answer questions related to the most important topics covered. My colleagues say this technique motivates some students to stay tuned in.]
- Ask students to compare their notes with each other in order to review the lecture and clear up any questions they may have.

With advances in technology, the use of clickers in lecture halls allows students to respond in class and immediately see how the class as a whole views a question or poll. Clickers fit into our students' desire for immediacy, instant feedback, and social connectedness.

Other technological advances include the use of exciting PowerPoint presentations with video clips from the Internet, and the wireless clip-on microphone allows the teacher to circulate in the lecture hall among the students.

Theater professor Morris Burns of the University of Texas outlines several such strategies derived from the field of acting:

- Bring more feeling into your presentation of ideas so that you show enthusiasm for what you're teaching. Being passionate about your subject is the best way to accomplish this objective. If you find yourself less passionate than you were when you began teaching, attend professional development workshops in your discipline so that you may recapture some of enthusiasm.

- Picture yourself successfully conducting your classes. Your imagination will pave the way for solid performance in the classroom.

- Use your voice in ways that are conducive to effective communication. For example, speak with inflection rather than droning on in a monotone.

- Use the way you move in class to project enthusiasm and connect with your students. For example, walk around the classroom and establish eye contact with students as you move.

- Think about the arrangement of your teaching environment. Check out, ahead of time, the room where you'll be teaching. Plan ways you can use the space to its best advantage—for instance, whether you should group students in circles or semi-circles.

- Prepare for class by thinking about not only the content you want to present, but also your students as audience members and individuals. Deliver your content in a way that is relevant to your students' lives by using examples they can relate directly to their everyday experiences. [This is easy to do in my discipline of psychology, but I've watched teachers in so many other disciplines—including mathematics—find ways for students to apply what they learn to their own lives.] (1999, 5-8)

Cleveland State University's Center for Teaching and Learning (Cleveland State University n.d) offers a guide, entitled *Active Learning for Almost Any Size Class,* with ideas for three alternative lecture formats:

1. *Feedback Lecture:* Two mini lectures separated by a small-group study session

2. *Guided Lecture:* A half-class lecture with no note taking, followed by a short period of individual student recall, and then a small group activity involving student reconstruction of the lecture with instructor assistance

3. *Responsive Lecture:* One class each week is devoted to answering open-ended, student-generated questions. Questions may or may not be submitted in advance.

Even with strategies to help make lectures more dynamic, we are still faced with what we have actually known since the time of Jean Piaget (1952) and John Dewey (1963): students learn more effectively by "doing" than by passively receiving pre-packaged information. In fact, the belief in the efficacy of active learning can be traced at least as far back as Confucius, the Chinese thinker and social philosopher (551 BC – 479 BC), who said, "I see and I forget, I hear and I remember, I do and I understand." And certainly the ancient Greeks were onto something when the philosopher Socrates (469-399 BC) used a form of questioning that has come to be known as the Socratic Method.

Of course more recently, we have study upon study showing that *doing* fosters more learning, retention, and higher-order thinking than passive listening.

Other research shows the ineffectiveness of the lecture method. (See Fassinger 1996 and Bligh 2000.) Roland Christensen (1982, xiv) colorfully states that traditional lecturing and note-taking is "like dropping ideas into the letter box of the subconscious. You know when they are posted, but you never know when they will be received or in what form."

The Community College Survey of Student Engagement has this to say about the relation between instructors' use of classroom time and student engagement:

Not surprisingly, more time spent on interactive instructional approaches appears to increase student engagement. For example, colleges in which instructors use high percentages of classroom time for lecturing have lower benchmark scores [according to national research of effective educational practices] *than those in which instructors spend high percentages of classroom time on in-class writing or small group activities.* (CCSSE 2009, 4)

The National Survey of Student Engagement (NSSE), *Assessment for Improvement: Tracking Student Engagement Over Time*, provides results from a 2009 survey of 360,000 students who attended 617 U.S. colleges and universities. It includes an in-depth look at trends in student engagement at more than 200 of those schools that had four to six year's worth of data going back to 2004. The 2009 report highlighted some signs of progressin relation to previous years:

- At institutions where faculty members report using effective educational practices more frequently in their classes (as measured on the Faculty Survey of Student Engagement), students are more engaged overall and gain more from college.

- Engagement yields larger payoffs in terms of grades and retention for underprepared students and historically underrepresented students relative to otherwise comparable peers.

- Certain high-impact educational practices and experiences correspond to higher student participation in deep approaches to learning.

Despite this supportive evidence on the productive role of active learning in the classroom, committed lecturers continue to protest. The lecturer's protest is one with which I am personally familiar. It reflects where I was a couple of decades ago: If my students are actively involved, class time is being taken away from what I have to tell them. I have to cover my course material in a limited amount of time.

I started to change from being a straight lecturer for a number of reasons. For one thing, as time went by, I was continuing to learn new things in my field and also learning that some of what I had been teaching no longer held true. My first approach was to try to teach students about the complexities of my field (psychology) by talking faster and faster. I was exhausting myself and one day I overheard one of my students tell a classmate, "I dropped my pen in lecture and missed a week's work." I realized that my students felt bombarded with information and were on overload.

Another thing that influenced my departure from straight lecturing was my participation in a retention study grant at my college. I started studying the retention literature and became more and more convinced that retaining students and helping them to earn a degree involved *engaging* them through *an active learning process.*

I also began to ask myself some revealing questions: I could lecture my way through my courses and thereby *cover* the material, but were my students *learning* what I was covering? Were they retaining the material? To use Bloom's (1956) language of higher order thinking, were they analyzing, synthesizing, and evaluating the material? Were they making what they learned their own by applying the material to real life situations? Were they creating anything new as a result of what they were learning?

There was yet another influence that pushed me to reconsider how I taught. My colleagues and I were engaged in groups that discussed what a college education is all about and what a degree should mean. The research literature from the 1990s and the first decade of this millennium suggested that the college experience should include inquiry and analysis, learning written and oral communications skills, developing critical and creative thinking, and developing informational and quantitative literacy. In addition, research said that students should become adept at teamwork and problem solving. How would I be able to expand my goals from teaching students about psychology to include what I was beginning to believe was a necessary part of a college education? There was only one way: Expand my teaching repertoire to include active learning exercises in the classroom.

Simple Active Learning Exercises

Paulson and Faust define the concept in their online monograph (2002, 1). They state:

> "Active learning" is, in short, anything that students do in a classroom other than merely passively listening to an instructor's lecture. This includes everything from listening practices which help the students to absorb what they hear, to short writing exercises in which students react to lecture material, to complex group exercises in which students apply course material to "real life" situations and/or to new problems.

Much of the following list (including explanations of active learning exercises) is adapted from Paulson and Faust's work.

Paulson and Faust start with a list of exercises that are geared towards individual student responses, rather than involving group work among students. Many of these exercises can be integrated into lectures or used between mini-lectures. Linda B. Nilson (2010) refers to these in-between exercises as *student active breaks*. They could include lecture note review and/or elaboration, solving problems, doing quick case studies, one-sentence summaries, and reaction/reflection paragraphs.

Some of the exercises discussed by Paulson and Faust can be used as formative assessments (2002); that is, they can help clarify what students are learning from presentations. Perhaps the most well-known and widely used activity is Angelo and Cross's "one-minute paper" (1993). The original Angelo and Cross questions were, "What is the most important point that you learned in class today?" and "What important question remains unanswered?" This latter was also known as the "muddiest point" question.

The instructor simply stops lecturing, asks students to respond in writing to the first question, gives them just one or two minutes to do so, and then repeats the process for the second question. Obviously, other questions could be used as well.

There is a variety of ways for the instructor to process students' responses. In my lecture classes of 200+ students, I would ask the first question and then circulate in the room and listen to what students thought were the most important points of the lecture.

To my surprise and delight, many students would say they had learned something that I had not actually said, but was the next logical conclusion. After listening to a handful of student responses, I would ask what the "muddiest point" of the lecture had been—what questions were unanswered for them. When I listened to a student describe a "muddy point," I would often ask another student to explain it. This whole process would take about five to seven minutes of my lecture time; it allowed students to integrate, and hopefully retain, what they learned. It also allowed me to assess what concepts still needed work.

Of course, some instructors don't process students' answers on the spot. Instead, they take home what students have written and start the next class with clarifications. That method works too.

Clement says to use *focus* activities or questions (2009). On the screen or chalkboard, write an activity or a question that students can begin as soon as they enter the classroom. These focusing activities can relate to the last class, reading material, or what will take place in the class that is about to begin. Clement further suggests putting objectives for the class session up on the screen or board; this will help you and students to stay on track and will help latecomers pick up what's going on and what they've missed.

Another technique that can work in some disciplines better than others is to ask students for their affective responses. Just as with the one-minute paper, the instructor asks students to respond to a question, but this time, he or she asks for an emotional or evaluative response to some aspect of the course content.

Similar to the affective response exercise is the *daily journal* assignment. Obviously, the affective response activity and the keeping of a daily journal give students the opportunity to explore their own attitudes and values. The daily journal can be an in-class writing exercise or a take-home assignment. It can be used in a host of ways.

My best use of the daily journal exercise occurred in a course I taught entitled, "The Psychology of Human Relationships." In that course, one of my goals was to make sure students did the reading assignments. I asked them to write something from their assigned readings before each class met. I also asked them to come to class two minutes early to participate in pre-class discussions on what they had read and written. I would come to class and do a silent roll call and then call the class to order after they had been talking for about five minutes. Thus, only three minutes of class time was devoted to their group journal sharing. When I started the full class discussions after they had shared something from what they had written, the conversation was the richest I had experienced in all my years of teaching. An additional benefit that I never dreamed would happen: One day I overheard one student say to another, "What do you mean you didn't read the chapter?! How do you expect to contribute to our discussion?"

Reading quizzes can serve a number of purposes. For one thing, they are another way to ensure that students read their assignments and come to class prepared. They can also help us determine what students are getting from the reading. Finally, if we ask the same sorts of questions on several reading assignments, students will begin to know what to look for when they read.

Clarification pauses are similar to the one-minute paper exercise. After a short period of lecturing, or following a particularly important concept, stop the class and ask if anyone needs clarification. During the pause, circulate room, look at students' notes, and answer students' questions.

Ask students to *reflect and respond in writing about their reactions* to a class demonstration or some other teacher-centered activity. You can provide students with prompts such as "I learned that. . ." or "I was surprised that..." or "I wonder about . . ." or "I most appreciated that. . . ." Getting students to reflect on what they've witnessed in class allows them to assimilate the lesson.

More *sophisticated questioning:* Teachers can enhance the effects of questioning as a teaching tool in order to increase student engagement and comprehension.

- The Socratic method, asking students to respond to questions during a lecture and challenging them to defend their answers, has some benefits and pitfalls. Students may stay more tuned in to the lecture because they know we will be asking questions.

- Calling on students at random and asking them to respond to questions they have not volunteered to answer is known as "cold calling." Proponents believe it is an effective way to keep students on their toes and opponents see it as unnecessarily causing students to be anxious in class. There is no absolute answer as to whether to cold call or not. I have seen some colleagues do it masterfully and others miss the boat. The masters always respond to students' contributions respectfully and use incorrect answers as teachable moments.

Weimer described some teachers' suggestions for making cold calling less "icy" (2009). In summary, we find that their ideas all involve establishing the expectation of student participation:

- Warn students that you will call on them without their volunteering. Discuss the importance of their active participation in the class.

- Attach a grade to participation.

- Provide opportunities for reflecting and responding—give students time to prepare. Use appropriate amounts of wait time. Maybe let students write some ideas and/or share them with another student first.

- Skillfully facilitate the discussion—set ground rules. Discuss what makes a "good" answer.

- Don't let a few students monopolize the discussion.

- Let students look at their notes or the text.

- Use questions appropriately—ask open-ended questions. Call on those students who might have relevant experiences or background knowledge.

- Create a supportive learning environment—let the classroom be a safe place where honest attempts to answer are supported and encouraged.

- Respond respectfully to students' contributions—use wrong answers as teaching moments. Get others involved in understanding misconceptions and errors.

Of course, another way to call on students is to *ask for volunteers*. When you ask students questions in class, choose your questions carefully. Occasionally, you might want to assess whether students "know the facts," but more often, pose open-ended questions that get students to think critically about the material. One strategy for encouraging more volunteers is to *increase your wait time* before calling on someone. Another is to get all students to *respond in writing* before calling on a volunteer. This brings in students who are reluctant to speak off the tops of their heads and cuts down on always calling on the same few people who volunteer repeatedly.

Another strategy that promotes active listening in class is to *ask students to summarize another student's answer*. If you do this regularly, students will heed what their classmates say rather than see another student's answer as a good time to let their minds wander.

The *Fish Bowl* is an interesting technique. Give students index cards to write down questions about the course material. They can put their cards into a big fish bowl either at the end of class or the start of the next class. You then pick out cards and answer the questions, ask the students to answer the questions, or alternate your answers with your students' answers.

Ask students to *create questions* for use on exams and quizzes. By asking them to create their own questions, you prod them to think more critically about course content. Additionally, the assignment pushes students to explore the major themes of the course and thus moves them to higher-order thinking.

All the strategies so far ask students to do something by themselves.

Strategies in which Students Interact

The following exercises get students interacting with each other in pairs.

Think/Write-Share-Pair (Angelo and Cross 1993): Ask students to think about and write a response to a question you pose. After giving them a minute or two to respond in writing, ask them to share their responses with a partner. Dyad work is more efficient than group work in that you save the time of establishing groups. Dyad sharing also gets everyone in the class talking to at least one other person. Another benefit is that when you later open the class to a larger group process by way of discussion, students are much more willing to participate.

Note Comparison/Sharing: By comparing their notes in class, students are able to assess whether they are getting the main points of the lecture. Students can then supplement their own notes with what they have learned from their partners. In the best of all possible worlds, students will continue this process outside of class.

Pairs of Students Evaluate Each Other's Work: Students are asked to complete an assignment at home, such as a short paper. The day the assignment is due, students submit their work to the instructor and give a copy to their study partner in class. Students give each other feedback on content, writing, and other factors depending on the nature of the assignment. Paulson and Faust underscore that this method is particularly good at getting students to improve their writing skills (2002).

According to McKeachie and Svinicki (2006), one of the best systems for paired sharing is what Marcel Goldschmid calls the *learning cell* (1971). The learning cell refers to a cooperative form of learning in pairs in which students alternate asking and answering questions on commonly read assignments.

Here is how the learning cell works: Students prepare questions from their reading assignments outside of class. At the start of the next class, students are randomly paired and partner A asks the first question. Partner B answers the question and some clarification may take place. Then they switch roles with B asking A the next question. Goldschmid and his colleagues (1974; 1975) found that the learning cell is effective in many disciplines, and King (1990) and Pressley et al. (1992) found that training students to generate thought-provoking questions enhances learning.

Students Working in Groups. Many educators and theorists use the terms "cooperative learning" and "collaborative learning" interchangeably, while others distinguish between the two types. In *Successful Beginnings for College Teaching: Engaging your Students from the First Day* (2001), I gave an extensive comparison of the two types of group work from a theoretical perspective.

One distinction between cooperative and collaborative learning characterized by Rockwood is the role of *power* in the classroom (1995a; 1995b). Rockwood says that cooperative learning is a structured student exercise, but with the instructor as the central authority. Students work together to solve a problem, for example, for which there is one answer. By contrast, collaborative learning entails power being shared among students and instructor. Students work together in small groups to reach a consensus on a problem or issue for which there is no one right answer.

For the purposes of this book, suffice it to say that the two types of group work, cooperative and collaborative learning exercises, have much in common and for that reason, I will use the terms interchangeably. In fact, other terms are often used to describe similar formats, as in problem-based learning, case studies, etc.

Let's first look at the criteria for effective small-group learning experiences. According to Johnson et al. (1991):

- Students have clear, positive interdependence. In other words, they depend on one another to complete a task.
- Students promote one another's learning and success.
- Students hold one another personally and individually accountable for doing a fair share of the work.
- Students use interpersonal and small-group skills, such as active listening and seeking clarification of other students' perspectives.
- Each group processes how effectively its members are working together.

Additionally, other characteristics of small group work are:

- Learners are active participants and teachers become learners at times.
- Learners sometimes teach.
- Everyone in the class is respected, diversity is celebrated, and all contributions are valued.
- Learners learn conflict resolution skills.

Johnson, Johnson, and Smith explain:

> The research on cooperative learning is like a diamond. The more light you focus on it, the brighter and more multifaceted it becomes. The power of cooperative learning is brightened by the magnitude of its effect sizes, but the more you read the research and examine the studies, the better cooperative learning looks. (1998, 32)

In their conclusion, Johnson, Johnson, and Smith reassure educators that:

Faculty who use cooperative learning are on safe ground. There is a rich theoretical base for cooperative learning. As the research has evolved over the past 35 years, five basic elements have emerged as critical to cooperative work in classrooms: positive interdependence, individual accountability, face-to-face promotive interaction, social skills, and group processing. The research evidence itself indicates that a) the theories underlying cooperative learning are valid and b) cooperative learning does indeed work in college classrooms. (1998, 33)

For those who are still skeptical, there are several meta-analyses and longitudinal studies that demonstrate the benefits of cooperative learning: see Springer, Sanne, and Donovan (1997); Felder, Felder, and Dietz (1998); Hake (1997); Winter, Lemons, Bookman, and Hoese (2001), to name a few.

The Nuts and Bolts of Forming Groups

The first issue is whether to divide up the groups yourself. What you do depends on your goals for the group work. If the same groups work together across several classes, it is often better to consciously create heterogeneous groups with regard to gender, race/ethnicity, and levels of academic performance. You can make it look random when you are creating the groups simply by asking students to join certain classmates. The additional benefit of having heterogeneous groups is that students can become more appreciative of diverse perspectives.

Further, not allowing students to self select is a good practice because students often choose to work with their friends in class. Not only is it more tempting for them to socialize than to stay focused on the task, but working with their friends doesn't allow for stretching beyond their comfort zones.

Silberman offers several suggestions for establishing random groups (1996):

- Use color-coded cards so that all students with the same color can work together.
- Use name tags of different shapes and colors to designate different groups.
- Use students' birthdays, with students lining up along a wall according to the month of their birth and then forming groups.
- Use playing cards with jacks, queens, kings, aces, etc. to form four-person groups (the optimum group size).

You could also have nameplates (large index cards folded lengthwise) with colored dots on them. An even simpler way to form random groups is to ask students to count, starting with the number one and ending with a certain number depending on how many groups will be forming. Then all the "ones" form a group, all the "twos," and so forth.

Whatever technique you choose (purposeful selection, random selection, or even self-selection by the students), there will probably be benefits to student learning. I say *probably* because as we all know, even the best intentions and preparation can't always make a technique work the way we expect it to.

Group-work Activities

Paulson and Faust suggest *posing a question* to be worked on in each small group (2002). Then the class can be re-convened and students can share their answers with the class as a whole. This technique can be used as an "Active Review Session" in which the instructor asks questions, students work on answers as a group, and then each group teaches "their answers" and leads a class discussion.

Students can *solve problems* in their small groups as well. They can use paper and pencil, the blackboard, or computers, and again present to the class. McKeachie and Svinicki say "Problem-based learning is [along with active learning, cooperative/collaborative learning, and technology] one of the most important developments in contemporary higher education" (2006, 221). The authors describe what they call guided design, the case study method, and simulations, all variations of problem-based learning.

To support the development of higher-order critical thinking skills, ask students to develop *Concept Maps* in their small groups. Concept maps are illustrations of connections between and among concepts or terms. Students develop maps by connecting related terms and concepts with lines. There are usually multiple connections. This type of exercise requires that students understand the concepts and organize them in order to establish meaningful relationships and see the bigger picture.

The creation of *Visual Lists*, either on paper or the blackboard, allows students to work together to identify comparisons and contrasts. One approach would be to ask students to draw a line down the center of the page and, together, list the pros and cons of a subject.

Jigsaw Group Projects were first used by the social psychologist Eliot Aronson in 1971. The school board of Austin Texas asked Aronson to help students adjust to the transition to desegregated schools. Aronson et al. created what they called the "jigsaw" classroom (1978), piggybacking on the prejudice reduction work of Gordon Allport (1954). Allport had found that two ingredients were necessary for reducing prejudice: groups of people must have equal status and must pursue common goals.

Aronson and his colleagues were striving to raise children's self-esteem and, at the same time, reduce prejudice (1978). To accomplish these, they put children in small desegregated groups. Each child was dependent on the others in his or her group to learn the course material to do well in the class.

To adapt this technique for the college classroom, you need to divide course material into several parts (but no more than five or six).

Assign your students to "home teams" with as many members as there are parts of the learning package. (Groups that are larger than five or six at the maximum become unwieldy and more susceptible to socializing.) Each home team member receives one part of the material to be learned—material in which he or she will become an "expert." Students then form "expert groups" with other members sharing the same material. Within these expert groups, students read and discuss the material until they have learned it well enough to teach it.

Next, these experts go back to their home teams and teach their part of the work to their team members. Jigsaw emphasizes interdependence in that each student can only learn all the material by learning from his or her classmates. Individual accountability is also part of the jigsaw technique since each student is tested independently.

McKeachie and Svinicki characterize it well when they state: "Students often learn more from interacting with other students than from listening to us. One of the best methods of gaining clearer, long-lasting understanding is explaining it to someone else" (2006, 219).

Another productive group-work activity is *role plays:* Students are asked to act out a part. In many disciplines, the material becomes more vibrant if students participate in role playing exercises. The exercises will work best if students have done the necessary research for their parts.

For example, Bair uses role playing in a mock trial in which undergraduates serve as expert witnesses and law students serve as their attorneys (2000).

Blatner says that role playing, a derivative of a sociodrama, is a method for exploring the issues involved in complex social situations (2002). He states further that role playing may be used for training professionals or in a classroom for the understanding of literature, history, and even science.

Similarly, *panel discussions* offer students the opportunity to be more than intellectually involved. Students are asked to do research individually on a topic and to prepare presentations as part of a panel. They present their material to the rest of the class. Each panelist makes a brief presentation and when they have all done so, other classmates can ask them questions. The keys for success using this method are to choose topics carefully, give students guidance for doing research, and develop creative ways to hold all students accountable.

Debates are another involvement technique. Debates can often spur student engagement and get them to analyze pro and con arguments. Sometimes it can be interesting to ask students to select a position on a particular topic that is at variance with what they believe. Giving them the opportunity to consider multiple perspectives fosters the development of critical thinking skills.

Games are fun ways to learn. There are too many possibilities for using games to list them all here. Some of my colleagues have used competitive teams to solve problems, with winners getting their solutions first on the blackboard.

McKeachie and Svinicki advocate using games because they both teach and entertain (2006). Many games are simulations of real-life problems. The early use of simulations often involved participants playing the roles of individuals or groups in some political or social situation. Now there are computer simulations and many of these are available in various disciplines. They are particularly effective at teaching science (simulated laboratories) and foreign languages. McKeachie and Svinicki write, "The chief advantage of games and simulations is that students are active participants rather than passive observers" (2006, 226).

To add spice to games in the classroom, some instructors offer *bonus points* that are added to final grades. Usually these bonus points have very little impact on the grade a student earns in a course but seem to be highly motivational nonetheless. The last decade has seen a big rise in instructors using games in the classroom.

One of the big proponents of *digital games* for college learning is Marc Prensky, an internationally known writer, speaker, consultant, and game designer. Prensky is the author of *Digital Game-Based Learning* (2001a). He explains why games are so engaging, what effects they have on learners, and the many purposes they can serve in classes[2].

The Learner-Centered Classroom

Since in the mid 1990s, there has been a "paradigm shift" in higher education. We've gone from traditional modes of instruction (i.e., the lecture) to less teacher-centered and more learner-centered modes. This moves the focus from what the instructor is doing to what students are doing and learning in class. The instructor moves from "sage on the stage" to "guide on the side." In the new learner-centered paradigm, effective teaching is about facilitating student learning and promoting positive learning outcomes.

In the interest of advocating the efficacy of learner-centered teaching, Wohlfarth et al. explain,

> The learner-centered paradigm departs from traditional teaching models by focusing on students more than teachers and learning more than teaching. Thus, classes are egalitarian; they emphasize critical thinking, active learning, and real-world assignments. (2008, 67)

In the learner-centered approach, students construct knowledge through gathering and synthesizing information and integrating it with the general skills of inquiry, communication, critical thinking, and problem solving (Huba and Freed 2000). Learner-centered instructors encourage students' reflection, discussion, and engagement. Also, they are able to create reliable assessments of students' mastery of content, often broadening assessment tools to include more varied learning evaluations.

Huba and Freed describe eight features that are considered the essence of learner-centered classrooms (2000, 33):

1. Learners are actively involved and receive feedback.

2. Learners apply knowledge to enduring and emerging issues and problems.

---

2 Prensky also includes an extensive list of URLs related to games in education on his website:http://www.marcprensky.com/dgbl/Prensky%20-%20Selected%20URLs%28web%29.h tm; c.f. Notre Dame's "Serious Games Learning Community," http://kaneb.nd.edu/programs/flc/ games/index.html.

3. Learners integrate discipline-based knowledge and general skills.

4. Learners understand the characteristics of excellent work.

5. Learners become increasingly sophisticated learners and knowers.

6. Professors coach and facilitate, intertwining teaching and assessing.

7. Professors reveal they are learners, too.

8. Learning is interpersonal, and all learners—students and professors—are respected and valued.

Maryellen Weimer's book, *Learner-Centered Teaching: Five Keys to Practice* (2002), greatly contributed to a clear view of what this pedagogy is all about. In a nutshell, Weimer outlines the key premises of learner-centered teaching:

1. Assume that students are capable learners who will blossom as power shifts to a more egalitarian classroom.

2. Use content not as a collection of isolated facts, but as a way for students to critically think about the big questions in the field.

3. Change the role of teacher from sole authoritarian to fellow traveler in search of knowledge.

4. Return the responsibility for learning to the students, so that they can understand their learning strengths and weaknesses and feel self-directed in their knowledge quest.

5. Utilize assessment measures not just to assign grades, but as our most effective tools to promote learning.

Using this framework, teachers become learners along with their students — there is a power sharing unlike the more traditional, authoritarian teacher model. The role of the instructor expands from being the content expert in the room to that of being of facilitator of student learning, what some have called an "educational architect" who designs learning tasks conducive to student participation.

There is still the instructional role of evaluator of students' work and performance. However, in the learner-centered classroom, formative assessments (feedback for the instructor) as well as summative assessments (grading of students' work) are used. Formative assessments, such as the one-minute paper, are used to guide instructors to improve the teaching and learning process.

Further, Weimer says that the role of the teacher is to guide learners using these seven principles (2002):

1. Teachers do learning tasks.

2. Teachers do less telling; students do more discovering.

3. Teachers do more design work.

4. Faculty do more modeling.

5. Faculty do more to get students learning from and with each other.

6. Faculty work to create climates for learning.

7. Faculty do more with feedback.

And the student's role changes as well. As Freire explained in his "banking theory," the student moves from being a passive recipient or empty receptacle into which the instructor "deposits" knowledge to being an active, engaged agent in the learning process (1970).

With a learner-centered approach, students must accept responsibility for their learning. The learner-centered paradigm fits very nicely with the current active-learning movement previously described in discussing what the best college teachers do (Weimer 2002).

To elaborate: Bain says that excellent teachers foster critical thinking, have a strong trust in their students, and are lifelong learners themselves (2004). In his words, the best college teachers "…don't teach a class. They teach a student." He offers several other characteristics of teachers who use learner-centered instruction; they:

1. touch the lives of their students

2. place a strong emphasis on student learning and learning outcomes through using varied forms of assessment

3. know their subject matter extremely well

4. are active and accomplished scholars

5. value critical thinking, problem-solving, and creativity

6. value teaching as much as research and consider it as demanding a challenge

7. believe that students want to learn

8. systematically collect formative assessments on their teaching

9. assess outcomes of their teaching and adapt as necessary.

Attesting to the wide acceptance of learner-centered teaching, the University of Southern California created a learner-centered task force. The task force drew on the work of Barbara McCombs, whose research examines both learner-centered education and assessment (1997; 1999).

McCombs's more recent work emphasizes the role of positive feedback between student and instructor, as well as the importance of a supportive and encouraging environment for learning, both inside and outside the classroom (2007). McCombs also suggests that instructors acquire a better understanding of students' perspectives on the learning experience and use diverse teaching strategies to encourage all students to be invested.

Parker Palmer's classic, *The Courage to Teach* (1998), captures the essence of the problem with traditional models, especially the lecture mode, which he says results in "teachers who talk but do not listen and students who listen but do not talk."

In addition, there is empirical research that supports learner-centered teaching. Wells and Jones (2005), for example, compared teaching informational systems development using a collaborative, learner-centered approach with teaching the same subject using the traditional method; they found students achieved better results with the former. Students in learner-centered classrooms not only earned higher grades but improved their ability to work collaboratively and took more responsibility for their learning.

The work of Steckol also supports the learner-centered paradigm (2007). Steckol assessed how the learner-centered strategy of using formative assessment improved student learning. In his study, students used the one-minute paper to summarize class material and they also created their own quizzes. Students in the learner-centered section of the course scored higher on the final exam than control group students.

The research of Wohlfarth et al. (2008) studied qualitative data (students' narratives of their own experience in learner-centered classrooms) and found support for all five of Weimer's key premises of learner-centered teaching. Thus, there is strong anecdotal, quantitative, and qualitative evidence that students learn better when fully engaged in the learning process.

Some Key Points for Learner-Centered Classrooms

- The focus of teaching and learning today isn't on what professors know but on what students take away.
- Course outlines – content is expressed in the form of Student Learning Outcomes: "The student will be able to…"
- Teaching, learning, and assessment are all connected and must align.
- The emphasis is on empowering students to take responsibility for their learning.

The challenge for instructors is to:
- Help students build on what they already know.
- Help them organize what they know.
- Help them think critically.
- Help them practice meta-cognition so they become aware of what learning strategies they use. Then they can monitor, evaluate, and maybe adjust their strategies.

Instructors should:
- Foster student-student interactions in class, particularly by creating collaborative learning exercises and learning communities.
- Set clear expectations about course requirements and coach students on the strategies that will lead to success. This encourages student motivation and commitment and promotes academic achievement.

Creating the Learner-Centered Classroom

One of the most important factors of creating learner-centered classrooms is getting students to buy into the approach. This may not be an easy. After all, many of our students are accustomed to lectures and note-taking and may be comfortable in that less active role, in which fewer demands are placed on them. Asking them to participate in learner-centered classes pushes many students outside their comfort zones. Understandably, they will want to know why we are rocking the boat.

Given the fact that we might meet with student resistance to the learner-centered paradigm, I believe it is important to talk about the research on teaching and learning with students. As Terry Doyle points out, there are three basic rationales of the learner-centered approach that may help the student buy-in process (2008).

The first rationale holds that new discoveries about how the human brain functions validate the paradigm shift to the learner-centered classroom. We now know that the dendrites of our brain cells only grow when the brain is actively engaged. We also know that neural networks formed in our brains only stay connected when they are used repeatedly (Ratey 2002). We need to explain how the learning tasks we are asking students to perform will facilitate the development of the neural networks that they need if they're going to be effective learners.

The second rationale holds that the skills students practice in class, such as collaborative learning in small groups, will help them in their future careers. It is in those kinds of activities that students develop active listening skills, problem-solving skills, and conflict resolution skills. These skills have become increasingly important for professionals in all fields.

Finally, the third rational holds that the learner-centered approach fosters the development of students' learning skills. Doyle says the learner-centered approach involves instructors helping students to (2002, 2):

- Learn how to learn on their own
- Develop communications skills needed to collaborate with others
- Take more control of their own learning
- Teach others
- Make presentations
- Develop lifelong learning skills
- Develop their meta-cognitive skills—know what they know, don't know, or misunderstand
- Develop the ability to evaluate themselves, their peers, and the teacher

Even if we clearly explain how they will benefit, students may still be skeptical about taking on the learner-centered approach. As Gary A. Smith says (2008), telling students why this approach is good for them is a little like our parents telling us to eat our vegetables for our own good.

If we show our own enthusiasm for the learner-centered approach and tell our students that we are committed to their learning and want them to have a valuable experience in our course, I believe students will respond positively. I think we will encourage their buy-in even more dramatically by getting them engaged in learner-centered discussions right from the beginning of the semester.

Here is an approach that met with much success: after greeting students and reviewing the syllabus on the first day of class, Smith projected this on the screen (2008):

> Thinking of what you want to get out of your college education and this course, which of the following is most important to you?
>
> - Acquiring information (facts, principles, concepts)
> - Learning how to use information and knowledge in new situations
> - Developing lifelong learning skills

Smith then asked his students to discuss these questions with their classmates, after which he asked for a show of hands as to what was most important to them. A rich discussion led to the conclusion that learners need to meet all three goals. I thought this was an effective way to begin the semester because getting student input fits in with the new learner-centered paradigm.

The Learner-Centered Syllabus

Another strategy many instructors use (and again, it fosters student buy-in) is to have students provide input into the course syllabus.

O' Brien, Millis, and Cohen say:

> Research on teaching and learning is consistent: the more information you provide your students about the goals of a course, their responsibilities, and the criteria you will use to evaluate their performance, the more successful they will be as students and the more successful you will be as a teacher. (2008)

Weimer suggests allowing students to have input into the creation of the entire syllabus (2002). Students can interview each other about what they want to learn and instructors can put their ideas on the board or newsprint. Using their input, the instructor brings a draft of the syllabus to the next class and together, they refine it.

O'Brien, Millis, and Cohen have an approach to the syllabus that is perhaps less revolutionary than Weimer's and thus more comfortable for many of us. They say that while the traditional syllabus is primarily a source of information that is too often distributed the first day of class and then ignored by students, the learning-centered syllabus is "an important point of interaction between you and your students in and out of class, face-to-face, and online" (2008, 11).

Indeed, O'Brien, Millis, and Cohen argue that the syllabus can accomplish far more than relaying basic information related to the course (2008). It can be used as a teaching and learning tool as well—conveying to your students your values about learning, setting a positive tone conducive to learning, and establishing what your students can expect from you and the campus community to support their learning in your course. As the authors put it:

> . . . composing a learning-centered syllabus is an important stage in the process of crafting educational experiences for your students. The process first requires a well-developed rationale concerning your personal beliefs and assumptions about the nature of learning and how it is promoted and produced. The process requires next that you establish what skills, knowledge, and attitudes you believe are of most worth, how they can be built into your course, and how they will be appropriately assessed. It requires that you create a learning environment for your students using teaching and learning strategies that are consistent with those beliefs. And finally, it requires that you compose a syllabus that will communicate your expectations and intentions to your students. (2008, 13–14)

The tone of the learning-centered course syllabus is important because you are trying to create an egalitarian classroom atmosphere. Encouraging words on how to be successful in your course can help with that.

Some of what you include in a syllabus is simply informational, that is, related to the logistics of the course: your name, office hours and location, email address, telephone ext., textbook(s), prerequisites, expected preparation and skills, supplies needed, topics to be covered, how students will be assessed and how final grades will be determined, what types of assignments are required and when they are due, campus services available (e.g., tutoring and writing centers), attendance and lateness policies, academic integrity policy, college services for the disabled, and statements about student conduct in class and on campus.

It is useful to solicit input from students regarding the syllabus, and particularly regarding the student behavioral guidelines portion of the syllabus. Behavioral guidelines, or guidelines for classroom decorum, have emerged mostly in response to the millennial generation coming to college. Millennials are so tethered to their cell phones and digital devices that many instructors see the need to have guidelines for their use (or non-use) in class. Oftentimes, behavioral guidelines also set limits on other class-room behaviors such as arriving late or walking in or out of class during an ongoing session. Asking students for their input is part and parcel of the learning-centered, egalitarian classroom, and once again, aids the process of student buy-in.

Going beyond logistics, O'Brien, Millis, and Cohen say the learn-ing-centered syllabus is used as a learning tool. The syllabus can show the logic and organization of the course. It can clarify instructional priorities and student and teacher responsibilities.

> The more we tell students about what to expect in a course by ad-dressing these details and removing from the syllabus and the course the unknowns and the guessing games, the likelier we are to enlist students' interest and cooperation. The syllabus be-comes an invitation to share responsibility for successful learn-ing. (2008, 22)

The fundamentals of developing a learning-centered syllabus require a well-developed rationale about your personal beliefs and assumptions re-garding the learning process itself and how it is facilitated. They will be re-flected as you establish what skills, knowledge, and attitudes are most important, how they can be built into your course, and how they will be ef-fectively measured.

A Word about Learn*er*-Centered and Learn*ing*-Centered Classrooms

O'Brien, Millis, and Cohen's book uses the term "learn*ing*-centered" rather than "learn*er*-centered." This is a rather important distinction. More and more educators are using "learning-centered" in their discourse to reflect the emphasis that has been spreading all across American higher education over the last decade and a half, and which has come to be called the *learning revolution*.

A leading voice of the learning revolution is Terry O'Banion. O'Banion is President Emeritus of the League for Innovation in the Com-munity College and Director of the Community College Leadership Pro-gram at Walden University. He led a significant plenary session at the

Summer Institute on Quality Enhancement and Accreditation in 2010. The purpose of the learning revolution, according to O'Banion, is "to place learning first in every policy, program, and practice in higher education by overhauling the traditional architecture of education" (O'Banion and Wilson 2010, 3).

In his address to the Institute, O'Banion used the metaphor of a "spa" to distinguish between *learner*-centered and *learning*-centered. Here is my paraphrase from memory (which will doubtless be less eloquent than O'Banion's original). Suppose a person went to a spa with the intention of losing five pounds in a week. And suppose the spa offered an array of services in a very friendly manner that would help him or her achieve that goal. There could be exercise classes, yoga, and delicious yet healthy food.

Now suppose the end of the week came around and the person had had a great time but hadn't lost a single pound. Obviously, the person did not achieve his or her goal. The spa was friendly, clean, safe, and provided all the necessary tools, but the objective was not reached.

In the same way, learner-centered classrooms can be designed with the best intentions, but if students do not achieve the learning outcomes, then the class is not a success. For teaching to be effective, learning must take place. So how do we know whether learning is taking place? This is where we need to be clear about our teaching goals, and clear about aligning learning outcomes with assessment tools.

Learning Outcomes and Assessment

Learning is the primary goal and focus of the learning-centered classroom. For this reason, assessment plays a crucial role in the move to the learning-centered paradigm. Because the focus is on learning, assessment in higher education is referred to as "outcomes assessment," "student outcomes assessment," or, most often, "learning outcomes assessment."

Huba and Freed define assessment as the process of gathering and discussing information from multiple and diverse sources in order to develop a deep understanding of what students know, understand, and can do with their knowledge as a result of their educational experiences; the process culminates when assessment results are used to improve subsequent learning (2000).

This more holistic view of the teaching and learning process places assessment at its heart. As Baud writes:

Teachers will need to become researchers of students' perceptions, designers of multifaceted assessment strategies, managers of assessment processes and consultants assisting students in the interpretation of rich information about their learning." (1995, 42)

There are two basic questions we need to ask ourselves in designing our courses and in assessing student learning (Weimer 2002):

1. What is it my students need to know and be able to do during their professional lives?

2. What skills and knowledge will stand the test of time, given the dynamic nature of knowledge and information?

Ruth Rodgers, teaching and learning specialist at Durham College/UOIT, in the recent online seminar entitled, *What to Teach When There Isn't Time to Teach Everything*, insists that in designing our courses, we need to identify the essential parts of our subject matter. Since we obviously can't teach students everything we know about our content area, we must decide what is indispensable, not only in terms of content, but also in terms of attitudes, processes, and lifelong learning habits that will help students to be successful in the field. Reflecting the learning-centered approach, Rodgers says it is more important than ever before that students develop the ability to evaluate, adapt, and apply information. She hears employers saying they are looking for college graduates with knowledge and skills, but equally important are students' abilities to analyze data and problem-solve.

So once we are clear about our teaching goals, we need to make sure that our assessments match our goals. Assessments can serve a number of purposes. They can:

• Improve student learning, instruction and the curriculum.

• Document successes and identify weaknesses in the course/program.

• Provide evidence of institutional effectiveness.

• Respond to demands for accountability from external constituents, as for example, the demands from accrediting institutions.

According to Huba and Freed (2000), two key questions should drive our assessment strategies:

• What have our students learned and how well have they learned it?

- How successful have we been at what we are trying to accomplish?

There is a movement from assessment *of* learning to assessment *for* learning, leading to more meaningful summative (grade-producing) assessments of deeper, more lasting, and higher-level learning (Taylor 2010). In teacher-centered classrooms, learning is assessed indirectly through the use of objectively scored tests. In the learner-centered paradigm, teaching and assessing are intertwined, assessment is used to promote and diagnose learning, and learning is assessed directly through papers, projects, performances, portfolios, and so forth (Huba and Freed 2000).

Formative and Summative Assessments

There are two kinds of assessments: *formative* and *summative*. In formative assessment, the goal is to gather feedback from students (e.g., *CATs*, Classroom Assessment Techniques) so as to improve instructional strategies (Angelo and Cross 1993). Summative assessments, on the other hand, attempt to measure the level of student success or proficiency by comparing students' work or performance against some standard or benchmark, with these types of assessments leading to final grades. Summative assessments are usually formal, comprehensive, and judgmental (see Carnegie Mellon n.d.).

The use of classroom assessments (formative) can be a terrific contributor to student learning. They provide you with feedback about how well the instructional methods you've chosen are accomplishing the task. Additionally, students get to evaluate how much they are learning and what is unclear to them, giving you the opportunity to clarify concepts.

Typically, testing and grading in teacher-centered classes involves students getting the "right" answers. In the new learner-centered paradigm, there is movement towards measuring other aspects of being a well-educated learner.

Huba and Freed pose the following questions related to our broader understanding of what it means to be well educated (2000):

- Can students gather and evaluate new information, think critically, reason effectively, and solve problems?
- Can they communicate clearly, drawing upon evidence to provide a basis for argumentation?
- Can students work respectfully and productively with others?

- Do students' decisions and judgments reflect understanding of universal truths/concepts in the humanities and arts?
- Do they have self-regulating qualities like persistence and time management that will help them reach long-term goals?

These authors say that for assessments to promote learning, they must incorporate feedback that learners can use in redirecting their efforts. Assessment information must, in other words, *reveal* to learners an understanding of how their work compares to a standard. Additionally, assessment must inform students of the consequences of remaining at their current level of skills/knowledge, as well as provide information about how to improve if improvement should be needed.

Weimer argues that teacher-centered practices place too great an emphasis on evaluation for purposes of grading, which has serious negative consequences for learning outcomes (2002). In the old paradigm, students are excluded from the assessment process because there are no opportunities for self-evaluation or peer-assessment strategies. Grades, Weimer says, often get in the way of learning. Learner-centered assessment changes that system.

Weimer further argues that learning could be enhanced by using more feedback that aims to improve the next performance. Effective feedback is directed at the student's performance and not at the student as a person. Immediate and well-timed feedback has the strongest impact. Feedback language should be more descriptive than evaluative.

The formative assessment process should include both self- and peer-assessment. Weimer explains that the linkage between the two is so tight that experiences in one area often contribute to the development of skills in the other (2002). For example, getting students involved in peer assessment sharpens their ability to assess their own work. Evaluating their peer's work teaches them how to critique and helps them develop confidence in their own judgments, especially if they can back up their evaluations with supporting data. Giving constructive feedback also helps them learn how to listen to and benefit from feedback on their own work.

Clearly written learning-outcomes statements are very important. They should be worded in such a way that they convey what students should be *able to do* by the end of the course. Learning-outcomes statements should be about performances that you can observe, set standards for, and assess, not about internal states of mind (Nilson 2010).

It is wise to align your assessment tools to your learning outcomes. Do the assessment tools measure learning outcomes that demonstrate student mastery? For example, although some researchers are finding ways for multiple choice tests to measure higher-order learning, short answer and multiple-choice tests typically measure whether students know factual information, while essay tests better measure higher-order thinking—i.e., analysis, synthesis, and reasoning (Pankratz, et al. 2004). So it is always a good idea to compare your assessment strategies with the goals you have for your students.

We need to be aware that grades (summative assessment) are probably the most anxiety-provoking aspect of a course for most students. Instructors can alleviate some of that anxiety and create grade-producing instruments that make sense to students and actually foster learning and retention.

Weimer offers suggestions for reducing the stress of summative grading experiences (2002). First, she says instructors can give students practice and prepare them for what they will have to do for the grade-producing evaluation; review questions, for instance, should reflect the questions on the actual test.

Paper assignments should allow students access to samples that illustrate appropriate topics and levels of treatment. Weimer poses this question, "Does it matter how long or how many tries it takes if students ultimately learn the content?" She says sometimes it may—but not always.

I am reminded of a remark one of my colleagues made many years ago at a faculty meeting where the discussion had to do with whether or not to set time limits for students to accomplish a task. My colleague was a professor of art. He said, "If time and speed are the main criteria for success, then Michaelangelo should have used rollers to paint the Sistene Chapel ceiling."

9 Principles of Good Practice for Assessing Student Learning

1. The assessment of student learning begins with educational values. Assessment is not an end in itself but a vehicle for educational improvement. Its effective practice, then, operates on a vision of the kinds of learning we value most. Educational values should drive not only what we choose to assess but also how we do so. Where questions about educational mission and values are skipped over, assessment threatens to be an exercise in measuring what's easy, rather than a process of improving what we really care about.

2. Assessment is most effective when it reflects an understanding of learning as multidimensional, integrated, and revealed in performance over time. Learning is a complex process. It entails not only what students know but what they can do with what they know; it involves not only knowledge and abilities but values, attitudes, and habits of mind that affect both academic success and performance beyond the classroom. Assessment should reflect these understandings by employing a diverse array of methods, including those that call for actual performance, using them over time so as to reveal change, growth, and increasing degrees of integration. Such an approach aims for a more complete and accurate picture of learning, and therefore constitutes a firmer basis for improving our students' educational experiences.

3. Assessment works best when the programs it seeks to improve have clear, explicitly stated purposes. Assessment is a goal-oriented process. It entails comparing educational performance with educational purposes and expectations—those derived from the institution's mission, from faculty intentions in program and course design, and from knowledge of students' own goals. Where program purposes lack specificity or agreement, assessment as a process pushes a campus toward clarity about where to aim and what standards to apply; assessment also prompts attention to where and how program goals will be taught and learned. Clear, shared, implementable goals compose the cornerstone of focused, useful assessment.

4. Assessment requires attention to outcomes and, equally important, attention to the experiences that lead to those outcomes. Information about outcomes is of high importance; where students "end up" matters greatly. But to improve outcomes, we need to know about student experiences along the way—about the curricula, teaching, and kind of student effort that lead to particular outcomes. Assessment can help us understand which students learn best under what conditions; with such knowledge comes the capacity to improve the whole of their learning.

5. Assessment works best when it is ongoing, not episodic. As a process, the power of assessment is cumulative. Though isolated, "one-shot" assessment can be better than none, improvement is best fostered when assessment takes the form of a

linked series of activities undertaken over time. This may mean tracking the process of individual students, or of cohorts of students; it may mean collecting the same examples of student performance or using the same instrument semester after semester. The point is to monitor progress toward intended goals in a spirit of continuous improvement. Along the way, the assessment process itself should be evaluated and refined in light of emerging insights.

6. Assessment fosters wider improvement when representatives from across the educational community are involved. Student learning is a campus-wide responsibility, and assessment is a way of discharging that responsibility. Thus, while assessment efforts may start small, the aim over time is to involve people from across the educational community. Faculty play an especially important role, but issues surrounding assessment can't be addressed fully without participation from student-affairs educators, librarians, administrators, and students. Assessment may also involve individuals from beyond the campus (alumni/ae, trustees, employers) whose experience can enrich the sense of appropriate aims and standards for learning. Thus understood, assessment is not a task for small groups of experts but a collaborative activity; its aim is wider, better-informed attention to student learning by all parties with a stake in its improvement.

7. Assessment makes a difference when it begins with issues of use and illuminates questions that people really care about. Assessment recognizes the value of information in the process of improvement. But to be useful, information must be connected to issues or questions that matter to individuals. This implies assessment approaches that produce evidence that relevant parties will find credible, suggestive, and applicable to decisions that need to be made. It means thinking in advance about how the information will be used, and by whom. The point of assessment is not to gather data and return "results;" it is a process that starts with the questions of decision-makers, that involves them in the gathering and interpreting of data, and that informs continuous improvement.

8. Assessment is most likely to lead to improvement when it is part of a larger set of conditions that promote change. Assessment

alone changes little. Its greatest contribution comes on campuses where the quality of teaching and learning is visibly valued and worked at. On such campuses, the push to improve educational performance is a prominent and primary goal of leadership; improving the quality of undergraduate education is central to planning, budgeting, and personnel decisions. Information about learning outcomes is seen as an integral part of decision making, and avidly sought.

9. Through assessment, educators meet responsibilities to students and to the public. There is a compelling public stake in education. As educators, we have a responsibility to the public, which supports or depends on us to provide information about the ways in which our students meet goals and expectations. But that responsibility goes beyond the reporting of such information; our deeper obligation — to ourselves, our students, and our societies—to improve. Those to whom educators are accountable have a corresponding obligation to support such attempts at improvement. (Astin et al. 1997)

Alternative Assessment Methods

The learner-centered approach requires that instructors stretch out of their normal grading patterns and become more creative. If our goals as teachers include encouraging authentic learning, critical thinking skills, and a deeper understanding of content—if, that is, we want our students to see the connections between the material and their lives and to develop greater abilities to engage in discourse around the content—the usual grading formats may fall short.

Brent Muirhead (2002), a leading voice in learner-centered teaching and assessment for online colleges and universities (whose work is certainly applicable to face-to-face instruction), says that using alternative assessment tools can encourage reflective thinking among our students. Self-directed learning and assessment activities can also encourage students to become involved in the personal construction of knowledge. Teachers can promote higher-order and critical thinking skills by having assessment tools that permit students to vary their responses to questions (Davies and Wavering 1999).

A popular alternative assessment tool is the *journal*, which was mentioned earlier as an active learning strategy for promoting reading and sharing. As an assessment tool, journal-writing assignments can be tied directly to the learning objectives of the course. When students keep reflective journals, all kinds of good things happen.

Muirhead lists seven benefits of journal writing (2002). Journals:

1. *Provide an aid to our memory:* researchers and writers have learned the value of recording their ideas for future use.

2. *Provide a basis for creating new perspectives:* journal writing creates a framework to explore relationships and arguments between ideas.

3. *Enhance critical thinking skills:* learning to analyze the underlying assumptions of our actions and those of others is a very liberating process.

4. *Provide psychological/emotional advantages:* journal writing enables individuals to work through difficult occupational or personal situations in ways that promote healing and growth.

5. *Offer opportunities to increase empathy for others:* individuals can address social issues and enhance their understanding of our society and world.

6. *Provide a practical way to understand books/articles:* writing creates a format to regularly examine reading materials and improve our ability to comprehend and recall knowledge.

7. *Provide support for self-directed learning activities:* journal writing requires personal discipline and establishing individual learning goals to complete journaling assignments.

Additionally, students keeping reflective journals tend to engage more deeply in the course readings. As an assessment tool, journals can give us insights into students' interpretations and evaluations of course materials. Muirhead insists it is essential for instructors to provide timely and constructive feedback on students' journal entries in order to help them make changes in their ongoing work—before submitting the next assignment.

Other alternative assessment approaches include grading oral presentations, panels, and debates. Portfolios of student work can also be effective summative assessments. Huba and Freed suggest various other assessment formats including papers and theses, projects, developing a product, some type of performance or exhibition, presentations of case studies, interviews, and clinical evaluations (2000).

Whatever assessment strategies you use, Muirhead says it is critical for students to be provided with clear grading criteria (2002). These should support high academic standards and be implemented with consistency. In order to accomplish those goals, it may be helpful to create *rubrics* for your students.

Rubrics for Grading and for Formative Assessment

A rubric, or scoring scale, shows how learners will be assessed and/or graded. In other words, a rubric provides a clear guide as to how "what learners do" in a course will be assessed. A rubric contains the essential criteria for the task and outlines the levels of performance associated with each criterion. Scores are assigned to reflect the degree of mastery within specific criteria.

McDaniel provides a clear definition of a rubric:

> A scoring rubric is a set of ordered categories to which a given piece of work can be compared. Scoring rubrics specify the qualities or processes that must be exhibited in order for a performance to be assigned a particular evaluative rating. (1994)

The Student Learning Outcomes Assessment Office at Rochester Institute of Technology (RIT) states that rubrics are scoring tools that explicitly represent the performance expectations for an assignment or piece of work (2011). A rubric divides the assigned work into component parts and provides clear descriptions of the characteristics of the work associated with each component at varying levels of mastery. Rubrics can be used for a wide array of assignments: papers, projects, oral presentations, artistic performances, group projects, etc. They can provide formative feedback to support and guide ongoing learning efforts, or they can be used in the summative grading process, or both.

In 1996, at Washington State University, The Center for Teaching, Learning, and Technology (CTLT), along with the General Education Program and the Writing Program, developed a seven-dimension critical thinking rubric. According to their framework, rubrics have three essential features: evaluative criteria, quality definitions, and a scoring strategy (WSU 1996).

Rubrics can be terrific assessment tools for students because they take the guesswork out of *how* an assignment will be graded. Thus, they may remove some of the stress of summative evaluations. The purpose of rubrics, according to Huba and Freed (2000), is to establish a set of instructional expectations and standards for the course and for particular graded assignments. Using well-designed rubrics will show how students' work compares to the standards set in the course. Additionally, rubrics offer students a vision of what the teacher wants to accomplish and why it is important. Here again, consistent with learner-centered philosophy, instructors can seek input from students in the creation of the rubrics for their assignments.

Analytic and Holistic Rubrics

Jon Mueller's *Authentic Assessment Toolbox* (Mueller n.d.) describes two kinds of rubrics—*analytic* rubrics and *holistic* rubrics. He explains when each should be used:

> For a particular task you assign students, do you want to be able to assess how well the students perform on each criterion, or do you want to get a more global picture of the students' performance on the entire task? The answer to that question is likely to determine the type of rubric you choose to create or use: analytic or holistic.

Mueller notes that most rubrics are *analytic* rubrics. An analytic rubric defines levels of performance for each discrete criterion. The instructor evaluates how well students meet a criterion on a task, distinguishing between work that effectively meets the criterion and work that does not meet it. When creating a rubric, you have to decide how fine a distinction will be made between different levels of performance within each criterion. It is usually better to start with fewer levels of performance, because the more levels you have, the finer the distinctions between them, and the more difficult it is to grade with consistency.

By contrast, a holistic rubric does *not* list separate levels of performance for each criterion. Instead, a holistic rubric assesses performance across multiple criteria and assigns a single grade that accounts for the whole picture. In other words, the instructor makes a judgment on how well someone has performed a task, considering all the criteria together—holistically—instead of separately. Each level of performance in a holistic rubric reflects behavior across all the criteria.

Five Key Aspects of Creating a Rubric

Huba and Freed outline five key points to be considered when creating a rubric (2000):

1. *Levels of mastery:* Achievement is described according to terms like excellent, good, needs improvement, and unacceptable.

2. *Dimensions of quality:* Assessment can address a variety of intellectual or knowledge competencies that target a specific academic discipline or involve multiple disciplines.

3. *Organizational groupings:* Students are assessed for multidimensional skills such as teamwork that involves problem solving techniques and various aspects of group dynamics.

4. *Commentaries:* This element of the rubric provides a detailed description of the defining features that should be found in the work. The instructor creates the categories for what is considered to be excellent, sophisticated or exemplary.

5. *Descriptions of consequences:* This is a unique rubric feature that offers students insight into various lessons of their work in a real life setting.

One of my colleagues, Dr. Carol Bork of Mercer County Community College, promotes using positive language to describe the criteria for each level of performance. In other words, you would state what students can do at each performance level rather than describe deficiencies.

Advantages of Using Rubrics

The Educational Technology Center of Kennesaw State University lists several advantages of using rubrics, which:

- Improve student performance by clearly showing students how their work will be evaluated and what is expected.
- Help students become better judges of the quality of their own work.
- Allow assessment to be more objective and consistent.
- Force the teacher to clarify his or her criteria in specific terms.
- Reduce the amount of time teachers spend evaluating student work.

- Promote student awareness about the criteria to use in assessing peer performance.
- Provide useful feedback to the teacher regarding the effectiveness of the instruction.
- Provide students with more informative feedback about their strengths and areas in need of improvement.
- Accommodate heterogeneous classes by offering a range of quality levels.
- Are easy to use and easy to explain. (Kennesaw State University n.d.)

In addition, Carnegie Mellon Design and Teach a Course: Enhancing Education notes that

Using a rubric provides several advantages to both instructors and students. Grading according to an explicit and descriptive set of criteria that is designed to reflect the weighted importance of the objectives of the assignment helps ensure that the instructor's grading standards don't change over time. *Grading consistency* is difficult to maintain over time because of fatigue, shifting standards based on prior experience, or intrusion of other criteria. Furthermore, rubrics can *reduce the time spent grading* by reducing uncertainty and by allowing instructors to refer to the rubric description associated with a score rather than having to write long comments. Finally, grading rubrics are invaluable in large courses that have multiple graders (other instructors, teaching assistants, etc.) because they can help *ensure consistency across graders* and *reduce the systematic bias* that can be introduced between graders.

Design and Teach a Course states further that rubrics can be used formatively to help instructors get a clearer picture of the strengths and weaknesses of students in their classes. By tallying up the number of students scoring below an acceptable level on each component of a rubric, instructors can identify those skills or concepts that need more instructional time and student effort.

A grading rubric helps instructors clearly communicate to students the specific requirements and acceptable performance standards of an assignment. When rubrics are given to students with the assignment description, they can help students monitor and assess their progress as they work toward clearly indicated goals. When assignments are scored and returned with the rubric, students can more easily recognize the strengths and weaknesses of their work and direct their efforts accordingly. (Carnegie Mellon, *Design and Teach a Course* n.d.). Rubrics fit in well to the authentic assessment philosophy and the learner-centered paradigm.

Technology Use in the Learner-Centered Classroom

The Learner-Centered Task Force at the University of Southern California (USC), in a paper entitled, Learner-Centered Teaching and Education at USC: A Resource for Faculty 2005-2006 (Anderson et al. 2005-2006), discusses the role of new technology in the learner-centered paradigm. Their description of the use of technology at USC mirrors what we see across the nation. Mixed media forms of instruction on college campuses include the use of PowerPoint, complex images and audio files, and of course, the internet.

Many instructors at USC and throughout the country post class materials on course websites. This is a terrific use of technology in that students can access materials whenever and from wherever they choose. Instructors would do well to monitor their students' responses to online materials because there is always the chance of negative unintended consequences, as for example, a drop in student attendance to class.

The use of PowerPoint is perhaps the most popular mainstream form of technology used in college classes today. If deployed well, it can broaden students' exposure to a subject through diverse visual information. Those instructors who are sophisticated in its use are able to incorporate video clips that complement the content. Another advantage of PowerPoint presentations is that they can be posted online on a course website. Here, once again, instructors must guard against their use by students as a substitute for class attendance.

On the other hand, PowerPoints that are done poorly (e.g., slides that are unclear and bombard students with words and more words) are often seen by students as *the new boring lecture.*

A recent technological development on college campuses involves the use of public response systems (PRS), or, as they are commonly referred to, "clickers." Clickers can be used in a variety of ways. Particularly useful in large classes,they allow instructors to poll students on an issue and then immediately present everyone's response.

As a formative assessment tool, using clickers can help instructors know what course material is clear to students and what remains unclear.

Instructors can use this immediate feedback to present 'muddy' material in a different way.

Clickers can enhance learner-centered instruction in a number of additional ways. The USC Learner-Centered Task Force notes that clickers (Anderson 2005-2006):

- Allow agility in teaching and immediate response to the needs of the class, as well as minimizing wasted class time.
- Engage students in active learning during class–students become true participants in the learning process.

The questions posed with clickers:

- Can be used to provoke thinking and to correct and challenge students' misconceptions.
- Can serve as launching pads for peer instruction.
- Can facilitate a more concept-based rather than skill-based course.

It is easy to see how some uses of technology can promote the learner-centered agenda. But technology can be a double-edged sword. For instance, laptops in class may help some students take notes more effectively, but may also be a distraction, with some students using them for social networking and playing games.

In "Technology Hasn't Helped Students' Study Skills," author Steve Smith cites recent research that suggests that students need to learn to use computers more effectively (2010). That research, conducted by Jairam and Kiewra (2010), found that students tend to study using computers much as they do using their textbooks. They over-copy long passages verbatim, take incomplete notes, build lengthy outlines that make it difficult to connect related information, and rely on memory drills like re-reading text or recopying notes.

Dr. Kiewra, an educational psychologist, suggests a more effective study approach that he calls the *SOAR* method: **S**electing key lesson ideas, **O**rganizing information with comparative charts and illustrations, **A**ssociating ideas to create meaningful connections, and **R**egulating learning through practice. According to Kiewra, SOAR more thoroughly complements how the brain functions.

Learning occurs best when important information is distilled from less important, when selected information is organized graphically, when associations are built among ideas, and when understanding is regulated through self-testing.

As with any other pedagogical tool, technology must be used wisely to promote student learning, and then must be carefully monitored and evaluated to ensure that it is serving a productive purpose: helping students reach learning outcomes.

Motivating Today's College Students—the Millennials

Millennials, the generation spanning the years 1982-2002, go by a several names. They are called "Generation M or Y," "Echo Boomers," or the "NET Generation." In the "Generation M" label, the M stands for Millennials. They are sometimes called Gen Y because they follow on the heels of Gen X. "Echo Boomers" refers to their number and the fact that many of them are offspring of Baby Boomers. And of course, the "Net Gen" term reflects the fact that they are the first generation to grow up with the Internet and to so thoroughly incorporate it into their lives. A PBS 2006 documentary referred to this group as *Generation Next*.

There is great interest in this generation. For one thing, they are significant in their sheer quantity. They represent roughly 39% of the American population and are equal to or have surpassed Baby Boomers (1946-1964) according to the Pew Research Center Current Population Survey (CPS) (2010). Figure 19 is a pie chart that depicts the new face of America.

As children of the Baby Boomers, this group is predicted to make up the bulk of U.S. population within 20 years. Experts say Gen Y ranges in size from 72 million to 78 million people nationwide and 2 billion worldwide (Alliance for Children and Families n.d.).

About 40% of young adults aged 18 to 24 were enrolled in either a two- or four-year college in October 2008. So far, about one in five Millennials are college graduates. An additional 26% are currently in school and plan to graduate from college, while an additional 30% are not in school but expect to someday earn a college degree. Younger Whites are about twice as likely as Blacks or Hispanics to have finished college (22% vs. 10% for both Blacks and Hispanics). But Blacks are significantly more likely than Whites or Hispanics to say they want to earn a college diploma (Pew Research Center 2010).

Another factor that makes Millennials interesting is that they are beginning to enter the workforce. The first of this generation graduated from college in 2002 and are entering the workforce just as the Baby Boomers are retiring. According to Larrabee and Robinson (2001), approximately

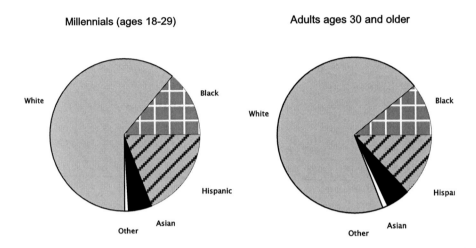

Figure 19: The New Face of America (PEW 2010). Reprinted with permission. Source:
http://pewsocialtrends.org/files/2010/10/millennials-confident-connected-
open-to-change.pdf

76 million Baby Boomers will retire over the next 25 years and only about 46 million Gen Xers are coming up behind them. This means that Millennials will influence the workforce for the next seven decades.

Millennials are the most diverse generation in our history — 45 percent are Latino, African American, American Indian, Asian, or Pacific Islander. They are the children of either Baby Boomers or early-wave members of Generation X. More than one in five has at least one immigrant parent.

Here is what we know in general about Millennials (keeping in mind that not every Millennial will fit this mold, for grand generalizations can never exhaustively describe individuals). A large number of them have been parented by Baby Boomers. How the Boomers parented was impacted by how they themselves were parented. In my training in family therapy, I learned about something called *systems theory* and how it can be applied to our understanding of parenting.

In family therapy, systems theory refers to the way families operate. Every family is a system with certain rules of communication and interactions that become patterns. Oftentimes, these patterns become so routine that people get stuck doing things the same way over and over and getting the same negative results.

There is good news and bad news about these ruts we tend to get into. The good news is that if we change, we compel others to change as well. Change in any part of the system produces change throughout the system.

The bad news is twofold—first, we can only change pieces of others' behavior, and second, when we change our behavior, the response we get back may not be the one we wanted. In fact, it may be worse than what we had in the first place. However, there is further good news: we can always change again, and again, and again, until we get a response with which we are more comfortable.

I mention systems theory in this context because according to the theory, people tend to parent the way they were parented. We do what we have learned to do. Not always: sometimes, we parent *opposite* to the way we have been parented. This happens often when we didn't like how we were parented but haven't done the hard work necessary to learn to do it *differently* but not necessarily oppositionally.

Here is a concrete example. One of my colleagues who taught a course in child development shared with me what happened in his class when he was trying to make this point (about parenting styles). A young man in the class, perhaps in his late twenties, challenged the theory. My colleague asked him to explain why. It turned out the student was a father; he shared with the class that his own father had had a very authoritarian style of parenting. He said his father would never allow him to express his feelings and always expected blind obedience. The student said, "In my family, I parent very differently from my own dad. He then said, *"My son will express his feelings!!!"* When he said this, other students smiled because they saw immediately that he was being just like his father.

Sometimes, however, people do parent opposite to how they were themselves parented by swinging the continuum way over to the other side. Here is another generalization: many Baby Boomers, who themselves were parented with strict and often authoritarian parents, since that was pretty common in those days, parented their children with a relatively permissive style. They wanted their children to communicate freely with them and share their feelings and therefore, many Baby Boomer parents negotiated with their children to empower them.

I see a lot of good in this style of parenting. However, some of these parents did not know when negotiations should come to a close. Perhaps related to this (we can't really say it is cause and effect), Millennials tend to be great negotiators. As educators, we may confront their negotiating abilities in the college classroom when some of them try to negotiate their final grades at the end of the term.

Millennials are the most protected and sheltered generation in history. Here is one example to show how times have changed: when I was three or four-years old, I had a steering wheel with a rubber sticker on the end of it that attached to the front windshield. As my father drove around, I "steered" while standing up in the front seat.

In contrast, Millennials grew up with the strictest government safety rules ever. Car seats, for example, must conform to the weight of the child and have safety buckles. As the child grows and gets heavier, so too must the car seat be changed to accommodate. One of my colleagues, a mother of four who is quite petite, mentioned one day that she is surprised there isn't government regulation for a car seat for her as she drives her minivan.

Perhaps the Baby Boomers are protective, and some would say overprotective, because they remember their own childhood and adolescent brushes with danger. And part of their protectiveness probably stems from their desire to keep their children safe in a world that is increasingly unsafe.

So, here is what we know about this Millennial generation as a whole. Millennials:

- grew up in a time of economic prosperity
- went to "play groups" from the age of three
- are the most protected generation in terms of government regulations on consumer safety
- were often indulged as a result of changing child-rearing practices
- are used to being consulted in decision-making by their parents
- typically have strong relationships with their parents, particularly with their mothers, and stay very connected, even when they go away to school
- are expected to excel by their parents
- were highly scheduled as children
- are in constant contact with friends via technology (Oblinger 2003)

Let's take a look at how some of what we know about Millennials may play out in the college classroom. We know that there are parental expectations for them to excel. Millennials have adopted this expectation for themselves.

When growing up and playing their "scheduled" games, very often, in order to make sure everyone's self-esteem would remain intact, there were prizes and awards for everyone. Baby Boomer parents wanted everyone in the group to feel included and successful, so all participants in an activity were told they were "special" and often given trophies for simply participating and making an effort (Carnegie Mellon 2008). Now these kids are in college and fully expect to get a A.

Many of my more recent students have said to me, "How did I get a B? I am an 'A' student!" Many of my colleagues have had long discussions with individual students and with classes as a whole trying to explain to them how grades are not merely about effort, as effort is not measurable.

If Millennials didn't excel in high school, and their parents had the financial means, many of this generation were given tutors, coaches, and classes that taught them how to do well (as for example, SAT prep courses). How does this impact their expectations in college? Many students expect individual attention, extra guidance, and institutional resources that will help them with any difficulties they encounter. Understanding this background may help ease the frustration some faculty feel about what they see as students' sense of entitlement.

Crone and MacKay say that students' priorities have changed due to increasing demands on their time from work, family, and emotional/ psychological needs (2007). Education, for many Millennials, has become commodified in a time of convenience and consumption.

A college degree for many of this generation is another acquisition to be made rather than a process of learning. Crone and MacKay point out how this is at odds with where students' minds need to be. They cite the work by the Association of American Colleges and Universities, *Greater Expectations* (AAC&U 2002). The AAC&U advocates that students need to become intentional architects of their own learning, actively setting goals, exploring, reflecting, and integrating acquired knowledge and experiences into existing world views. The question remains, "How can today's faculty inspire students to move beyond commodity thinking and become fully engaged in leaning?"

Understanding the entitlement background helps us gain a better understanding of those students who may *not* have this mentality, such as most (though not all) of my students in the community college sector. I've found that low-income, first generation to college, and minority students rarely express a sense of entitlement and rarely expect themselves to excel the way White Millennials do.

Much of the research on Millennials and the findings that are now widely disseminated focus on middle-class Millennials. These are students who seem to be very attached to their parents, and the feelings are mutual. Hispanic students are also very attached to their families, but a majority of Hispanic students attend community colleges while living at home.

At residential colleges, when we see students walking across campus talking on their cell phones, they are often in conversation with one of their parents. There have been many recent news articles about parents having difficulty leaving their children when they take them to college. Some institutions have established "goodbye" ceremonies and set limits on how long parents can stay.

One news article said that it was not uncommon for parents to book a room at a nearby hotel for the night so they could see their child one more time before leaving for home. One mother accompanied her daughter to the first day of classes and then went to the registrar to try to have her daughter's schedule changed. This type of phenomenon is seen so often that many over-involved parents are referred to as "helicopter" parents for hovering over their children, or "velcro" parents for not letting them go.

Prensky has dubbed this generation *digital natives* (2001b). He means that this generation was raised in a technological environment and accepts that environment as the norm. They have grown up surrounded by digital devices and use these devices regularly to interact with other people and the outside world.

Millennials have never known a world without computers; for them—except, perhaps, for some students from lower socioeconomic backgrounds—computer technology is an assumed part of life. Millennials have always used the internet as their first source of information, even before textbooks. They also use the internet for interactivity and socializing and for playing games, preferring the computer to television.

Moreover, cell phones are among their most essential tools. Millennials need to stay connected with friends and family *all the time*. They are often referred to as the "always connected" generation. The Pew Research Report says,

> More than eight-in-ten say they sleep with a cell phone glowing by the bed, poised to disgorge texts, phone calls, emails, songs, news, videos, games and wake-up jingles. (2010, 1)

Cell phones are almost like bodily appendages for this generation. It seems Millennials are constantly talking on their cell phones or using them to send text messages. In fact, "texting" has superseded using the phone to actually talk with someone.

In an article entitled, "Kaiser Study Shows Media Use by Youth is Heavy and Rising," I reported on some related findings (McGlynn 2010). The Kaiser Foundation report found that from 1999 to 2009, the use of digital devices for social connection and entertainment, even for middle schoolers, has skyrocketed (Rideout 2010). Media use for entertainment among our young has risen dramatically (Rideout 2010), especially among 11 to 14-year-olds and minority youth (see Figure 20).

Two findings from the Kaiser report about the heaviest media users were particularly disconcerting. The first is that media usage increases dramatically when children become "tweens," the 11 to 14 age range. When they hit the tweens, their time spent watching TV increases almost an hour and a half per day. Time spent listening to music increases about an hour and a quarter. Computer time goes up an hour and playing video games increases 24 minutes. This equates to a total media exposure of 11 hours and 53 minutes a day compared to 7 hours, 51 minutes a day for eight to 10 year-olds.

The study found that tweens and teens report spending an average of one and a half hours a day sending and receiving text messages. The study did not count texting as entertainment media.

The second disheartening finding was that Black and Hispanic children spend far more time with media than White children do. The results show:

- Black and Hispanic children consume nearly 4 and a half hours more media daily.
- For total media exposure, Hispanics report 13 hours a day, Blacks report a close 12 hours, 59 minutes, and Whites report 8 hours, 36 minutes a day.

Some of the largest differences occurred for TV viewing:

- Black children (tweens and teens) spend nearly six hours watching TV daily.
- Hispanic tweens and teens spend just under five and a half hours watching TV.
- For white tweens and teens, the 2009 amount of TV time was 3 hours, 36 minutes.

In a typical day, average amount of time spent with:			
	AGE		
	8-10	11-14	15-18
TV content	3:41	5:03	4:22
Music	1:08	2:22	3:03
Computers	:46	1:46	1:39
Video games	1:01	1:25	1:08
Print	:46	:37	:33
Movies	:28	:26	:20
TOTAL MEDIA EXPOSURE	7:51	11:53	11:53
Multitasking Proportion	30%	27%	30%
TOTAL MEDIA USE	5:29	8:40	7:58

Figure 20: Time Spent with Media, by Age.
Source: Kaiser Report (2010, 37). Reprinted with permission.

Differences by race/ethnicity remain even after controlling for factors such as age, parents' levels of education, and single versus dual-parent homes. This race/ethnicity disparity has increased substantially over the last five years from 2 hours, twelve minutes in 2004 to 4 hours, twenty-three minutes today.

Today's students from all backgrounds have spent their entire lives surrounded by and using computers, videogames, digital music players, video cams, cell phones, and all the other toys and tools of the digital age. Today's average college grads have spent less than 5,000 hours of their lives reading, but over 10,000 hours playing video games (not to mention 20,000 hours watching TV).

Multitasking is a way of life for this generation. High levels of multitasking were found in the Kaiser study. About 40% of the population surveyed say they use another medium "most" of the time they are listening to music, using a computer, or watching TV.

Wallis et al. say that the Millennials seem to have mastered multi-tasking in ways that previous generations either admire or disparage (2006). Millennials can be found listening to their iPods, doing their home-work, texting, and posting online messages all at the same time. Although some people see this ability as an asset and believe that Millennials' brains have been altered by experience so that they can actually multitask, many cognitive psychologists say Millennials are sacrificing the quality of their attention by doing two or more things at once.

Neuroscientist Jordan Grafman, chief of the cognitive neuroscience section at the National Institute of Neurological Disorders and Stroke, says of multitasking: "You're doing more than one thing, but you're ordering them and deciding which one to do at any one time" (Wallis et al. 2006, 52). The term cognitive psychologists use for this phenomenon is "cognitive toggling."

What are the implications of multitasking for this generation? They are probably sacrificing concentration and focus on their studies. How can instructors help them? Maybe if we explain the concept of cognitive toggling to them and tell them they would be much more efficient in their study time if they concentrate only on studying, some of them will heed our advice.

Skiba and Barton say since Millennials have little tolerance for delays due to growing up in a 24/7 world (2006), it is important for instructors to let students know when they can expect feedback or a response to their queries. They also say that the idea of constructing knowledge within a social community has lots of appeal to this generation.

More generalizations: Millennials tend to be conventional, accepting of societal rules and expectations. They tend to be team oriented. Although they are achievement oriented, they tend to have an external locus of control, that is, they are likely to place responsibility for their learning outside themselves. It is not surprising to meet Millennial students and workers who are ambitious but unrealistic. Given this, part of the instructor's task is to help them take responsibility for their own learning and to become self-regulators and self-monitors.

Millennials are often intellectually naïve, that is, they need help determining reliable sources of information. This is why so many colleges and universities are emphasizing information literacy across their curricula.

Using What We Know
to Motivate Millennials

The prerequisite for motivating Millennials, and other generations of students as well, is *engagement*. Throughout the early part of this chapter, we looked at two factors that seem especially important in engaging this group of students. The first is *social connectedness* and the second is the *use of active learning strategies*.

Given what we know about Millennials, here are some tips that can help us engage and motivate them:

- Provide students with *high, clear expectations*. Millennials want structure. They want to know what to do and how to do it so they can be successful. Expect high achievement from them and then guide them to get there.

- Offer frequent and ongoing *feedback*. Where it is appropriate, engage them through *technology* and social networking. I say "where appropriate" because we know that technology must be well used in our educational goals and not just used for the sake of using it.

- Millennials are *team players*. Many of them have played in groups since they were toddlers. Use that propensity for group activities to engage them through collaborative and cooperative learning exercises.

Smetanka found that today's college students want us to have high energy in the classroom and to be passionate about both our subjects and our teaching (2004). They want us to be creative, humorous, active, and entertaining. Some of us may balk at these notions. We are teachers, we say, not stand-up comics. Yes, but unless we work the room and every student in it, this generation will probably tune us out.

Pascarella and Terenzini state that millennial students need their instructors to be clear, well organized, approachable, available, engaging, and able to manage class time effectively (2005).

Clement says we should have a four-step plan for every class (2009):

1. *Set goals* for each class.

2. *Focus* the students and *present new material*.

3. Get students to *apply the course material* or *do something creative* with it.

4. *Review, conclude*, and *assess*.

The Center for Teaching at Vanderbuilt University offers the following research-based strategies for motivating students to learn (Vanderbilt University 2010). They base their compilation on the research of Bain (2004), Nilson (2003), and DeLong and Winter (2002).

1. *Become a role model for student interest.* Deliver your presentations with energy and enthusiasm. As a display of your motivation, your passion motivates your students. Make the course personal, showing why you are interested in the material.

2. *Get to know your students.* You will be able to better tailor your instruction to the students' concerns and backgrounds, and your personal interest in them will inspire their personal loyalty to you. Display a strong interest in students' learning and a faith in their abilities.

3. *Use examples freely.* Many students want to be shown why a concept or technique is useful before they want to study it further. Inform students about how your course prepares students for future opportunities.

4. *Use a variety of student-active teaching activities.* These activities directly engage students in the material and give them opportunities to achieve a level of mastery.

   - Teach by discovery. Students often find it satisfying to reason through a problem and discover the underlying principle on their own.
   - Cooperative learning activities are particularly effective as they also provide positive social pressure.

5. *Set realistic performance goals* and help students achieve them by encouraging them to set their own reasonable goals. Design assignments that are appropriately challenging in view of the experience and aptitude of the class.

6. *Place appropriate emphasis on testing and grading.* Tests should be a means of showing what students have mastered, not what they have not. Avoid grading on the curve and give everyone the opportunity to achieve the highest standard and grades.

7. *Be free with praise and constructive in criticism.* Negative comments should pertain to particular performances, not the performer. Offer nonjudgmental feedback on students' work, stress opportunities to improve, look for ways to stimulate advancement, and avoid dividing students into sheep and goats.

8. *Give students as much control over their own education as possible.* Let students choose paper and project topics that interest them. As-

sess them in a variety of ways (tests, papers, projects, presentations, etc.) to give students more control over how they show their understanding to you. Give students options for how these assignments are weighted.

With all the attributes instructors must have to be effective college teachers, being inspiring and able to motivate students probably tops the list.

Chapter 3 looks at the role institutions of higher education, high schools, and state governments can play in promoting degree completion.

Tool Box

For more research on the benefits of *active learning pedagogy* for underrepresented and underprepared students, see: Kraemer 1997; Cummings 2001; McGlynn 2007c, 2007d, 2008a, 2008b.

For research supporting the *"community" findings*, see Freeman, Anderman, and Jensen 2007; Bank, Slavings, and Biddle 1990; Frost 1999; and Padilla 1999.

For a list of *icebreakers*, see McGlynn 2001, Magnan 2004, Downing 2010, or On Course n.d. Strategies.

For studies on *"doing"* as a learning enhancer, see McKeachie and Svinivki (2011, 2006); Prince (2004); Pascarella and Terenzini (2005; 1991); Milton, Pollio, and Eison (1986); Thompson, Licklider, and Jungst (2003); Blumberg (2007); Bain (2004); Johnson, Johnson, and Smith (1991); Bransford, Brown, and Cocking (1999); McKeachie, Pintrich, Yi-Guang, and Smith (1986); Bonwell and Eison (1991).

For a discussion on students becoming adept at *teamwork and problem solving*, see National Leadership Council for Liberal Education and America's Promise 2007.

For an interesting and in-depth discussion of *cold calling*, see Dallimore, Hertenstein, and Platt (2004).

Another wonderful source on *cooperative and collaborative learning* is Educational Broadcasting Corporation, 2004.

In the new learner-centered paradigm, effective teaching is about *facilitating student learning and promoting positive learning outcomes*. See American College Personnel Association 1996; Angelo 1997; Barr and Tagg 1995; and On Course n.d.

Jon Mueller's *Authentic Assessment Toolbox* (n.d.) can give further guidance in creating rubrics.

See also a discussion on clickers by Tom Haffie, "Broadcollecting: Using Personal Response Systems ("Clickers") to Transform Classroom Interaction" (2010).

Chapter 3

Improving Graduation Rates through Institutional Commitment

In chapter 1 we identified the problem: too few young people are earning postsecondary credentials. America is not producing enough associate's degree completers, awarding enough postsecondary certificates, or educating enough bachelor's degree recipients to remain competitive in a global economy. Given the demographic shifts in our society, we must graduate more low-income, African American, and Hispanic students, and close the White / low-income, first-generation, minority students' achievement gap, in order to remain competitive in a global economy and meet the future needs of the job market.

In chapter 2 we explored what college instructors can do to help *all* students become more successful. The research shows that what helps all students tends to be particularly helpful to underserved populations.

The things faculty can do to promote student success are pretty straightforward: anything that enhances student engagement and supports social connections is on track.

When we look at the responsibilities of institutions of higher education, including the responsibilities of their leaders, the waters get muddied.

Swail, Redd, and Perna's work, *Retaining Minority Students in Higher Education: A Framework for Success* offers a geometric model relating to student persistence (2003). Picture a triangle. The three sides are labeled:

cognitive factors, social factors, and institutional factors. At the center of the triangle is the student experience. This model recognizes that students bring to campus certain attributes, and these attributes are one part of a larger picture of their experience. "Institutional factors" are placed at the base of the triangle, indicating their foundational contribution to academic success.

Tinto's numerous studies on retention emphasize the importance of social and academic integration for student success (1994; 1998; 2003). The retention literature demonstrates that peer relations, role models, and mentors are significant variables when it comes to academic success.

Tinto's "Model of Institutional Departure," the seminal work on retention, identifies three major sources of student departure: academic difficulties, the inability of individuals to resolve their educational and occupational goals, and individuals' failure to become or remain incorporated in the intellectual and social life of the institution.

Tinto's model says that in order for students to persist to a degree, they need to become integrated into formal (academic performance) and informal (faculty/staff interactions) academic systems, and formal (extracurricular activities) and informal (peer-group interactions) social systems.

In a paper delivered at Staffordshire University, Tinto says,

Five conditions are known to promote persistence. These are expectations, support, feedback, involvement, and learning. (2003, 2)

This chapter will look at the role of factors outside the student that can impact his or her performance.

Moore and Shulock emphasize the role of institutions and their decision makers in creating a supportive environment:

Action to increase completion for all students and reduce racial/ethnic disparities must occur on two mutually supportive fronts: changes to institutional practices at the college level and changes to state and system policy. Both rely on the strategic use of data to track student milestone achievement and enrollment patterns. (2010, iii)

Institutional factors include the practices, strategies, and culture of the college or university, which, "in an intended or unintended way, impact student persistence and achievement" (Swail, Redd, and Perna 2003, 77).

Swail, Redd, and Perna emphasize that issues such as course availability, content, and instruction all affect student persistence (2003). So do support mechanisms such as tutoring, mentoring, and career counseling. Not only do the institutional factors mentioned above provide the foundation for academic persistence and success, they are also flexible enough to meet the diverse needs of all student populations.

The report by *Public Agenda,* referenced earlier in chapter 1, suggests some simple institutional changes. Students who did not finish college pointed to structural changes that would have been helpful and would have made it possible for them to continue. From the report:

> Much of the broad national discussion about raising college completion rates has focused on making loans more available and keeping tuition costs in line. But the vast majority of young people who made the decision to leave college without a degree (or, in effect, had the decision made for them by circumstances) point first to options that would give them more flexibility in schedules and help them mitigate the challenge of working and going to school at the same time. Eight in 10 of those who did not complete college supported two proposals that they believe would make college graduation feasible:
>
> 1. Making it possible for part-time students to be eligible for more financial aid (81% said this would help "a lot"); and
>
> 2. Offering more courses in the evening and on weekends so that they could continue working while taking classes (78% said this would help "a lot"). (Johnson et al. 2009, 18)

Tackling all the theories about retention is beyond the scope of this book. Instead, I'll try to distill some of the "best practices" from many resources that lay out the complexities of the issues. This chapter points to those resources as a guide.

Since level of preparedness is a key factor in college success, institutions of higher education must be involved in educational reform of the K-12 sector. The Education Trust mentioned in chapter 1, established in 1990 by the American Association for Higher Education to support K-12 reform efforts, does exactly that.

In preparing students to attend college and offering them access, persistent disparities must be addressed. *Measuring Up 2008: The National Report Card on Higher Education* describes some of them (NCPPHE 2008a):

- The high school graduation rate has decreased over the past 20 years for all racial and ethnic groups, with large gaps apparent among groups. The national on-time high school graduation rate was 77.5% for all students. For African American students, the high school graduation rate was 69.1% and for Hispanic students the rate was 72.3%.

- A growing number of high school students are taking longer to complete their studies or are dropping out of high school without a diploma. Among those who drop out, some students earn GEDs, but these students are less likely to enroll in college and if they do enroll, they are less likely to complete a certificate or degree.

- Disparities in college access are closely linked to race/ethnicity and income. In terms of race/ethnicity, 73% of White students, 56% of African American students, and 58% of Hispanic students enroll in college the fall following their high school graduation.

- Disparities in college enrollment based on income are stark: 91% of high school students from families earning above $100,000 enroll in college. From middle-income families (those earning $50,000 to $100,000), 78% enroll in college. In the lowest income group ($20,000 and below), the rate is 52%.

Provide Rigorous High School Curricula

Where do we begin to address these inequities? Colleges and universities can (and many are already doing this) work with their local high schools to implement more rigorous high school curricula. One useful strategy is to have faculties in both sectors do joint professional-development training to share best practices in instruction. High school students must learn the basics in high school and must be prepared to do college-level work. High school curricula need to place more emphasis on teaching critical thinking skills and on developing writing skills.

Students should leave high school proficient in quantitative skills as well. In fact, taking advanced mathematics in high school has been found to increase the chances that low-income, first-generation students will attend college, particularly four-year institutions (Choy 2001; Horn and Nuñez 2000).

A statement from the National Conference of State Legislatures notes:

> Research shows that successful high schools provide rigorous academic coursework, relevant learning opportunities, and meaningful relationships with instructors who are qualified to help students achieve high standards. (NCSL 2008)

The NCSL article goes on to say that a rigorous high school curriculum is one of the best predictors of whether a student will graduate from high school and earn a college degree. The U.S. Department of Education found that the rigor of high school course work is more important than parent education level, family income, or race/ethnicity in predicting whether a student will earn a postsecondary credential.

Unfortunately, recent research has shown that a majority of high school students don't feel challenged by their high school course work. A rigorous high school curriculum would offer challenging instruction and provide support for each student to meet high standards. To meet high standards, there needs to be support for low-performing students through intervention programs and extended learning opportunities. Additionally, each student should be required to complete a college- or work-ready curriculum in order to graduate from high school.

Furthermore, research has shown that (NCSL 2008):

1. Aligning high school standards to college and workplace expectations is a critical step toward giving students a solid foundation in the academic, social, and workplace skills needed for success in postsecondary education or a career.

2. Students who are adequately prepared for postsecondary education are unlikely to require remedial classes in college, a key indicator for college success. Although approximately 45% of all students who enroll in postsecondary education will ultimately earn a bachelor's degree, only 17% to 39% of students who take remedial courses will successfully earn that degree, depending on the number and type of remedial courses taken. Among students who take no remedial courses, 58% will earn a bachelor's degree.

3. The American Diploma Project has found that there is a common core of knowledge and skills—particularly in English and math—that students must master to be prepared for both postsecondary education and well-paying jobs. The research shows

that there is a strong correlation between scores in high school math and English and wages earned once in the workplace. Students who are taking below-average or functional/ basic English increase their likelihood of being employed in a low-paid or low-skill job. Students in the top quartile of mathematics scores earn significantly more in the decade following high school than do students in the lower quartiles.

NCSL Research shows that creating multiple pathways to graduation through a variety of learning opportunities provides students with ways to link subject areas with both personal experiences and the work world. Relevant learning opportunities could include in-depth projects that take place both in the classroom and the work place, internships, or community partnerships.

New research has also found that *personalized learning*, i.e., learning that includes a combination of courses and experiences that match the needs and interests of each student, is motivational and aids retention.

Offer College Courses to High School Students

Allowing (and encouraging) students to take college courses in high school has been found to increase high school graduation rates and college completion rates by giving students information about the skills they'll need to do well in college. High school students who take college courses are better prepared when they enter college and can use their credits to offset their college tuition by shortening their stay in college.

Promote Social Connections

Students perform better in high school when they they have a personal relationship with a caring adult. High school retention is improved if students connect with their teachers, other adult staff, and their principals.

When teachers and students have meaningful relationships, both are motivated to make the high school environment successful.

Enhance College Readiness

Not being ready for college is a widespread problem, particularly at less selective institutions of higher education. There are three types of postsecondary institutions: highly selective four-year institutions, somewhat selective four-year institutions, and nonselective or open-access two-year colleges. In the most selective universities, the readiness gap is negligible because admissions criteria screen out most students who are under-prepared to do college-level work. However, in the other two sectors of higher education, where 80% to 90% of students enroll, the eligibility-readiness gap is huge. Figure 21, derived from *Beyond the Rhetoric: Improving College Readiness Through Coherent State Policy* shows the extent of the prob-lem by illustrating the gap between eligibility for college and readiness to do college-level work (Shulock et al. 2010).

The community college sector typically requires only a high school di-ploma or the GED equivalent of a diploma in order to be admitted. Ap-proximately 75% of those admitted need remedial work in English, mathe-matics, or both.

Less selective four-year institutions (often the state colleges) typically require a high school diploma, additional college-preparatory coursework, and various other requirements related to grades and SAT scores. And yet, about half of incoming first-year students are still underprepared for col-lege-level work. Estimates are that as many as 60% of incoming freshmen require some remedial instruction.

According to *Beyond the Rhetoric*, "the college readiness gap reflects the disparity between the skills and knowledge that students gain in high school versus the skills and knowledge that colleges and universities ex-pect" (Shulock et al. 2010, 3). The report further explains that the gap be-tween what high schools teach and what colleges expect will persist as long as the two sectors do not develop expectations jointly. Complicating the situation is the diffuse nature of readiness standards within college and university systems.

Beyond the Rhetoric says systemic readiness reform can be achieved only if all of the factors that affect what teachers teach and what students learn are in place and are coordinated around mutually accepted statewide col-lege readiness standards. These factors include the standards themselves and the application of the standards through teacher preparation and training, high school assessments and curriculum, college placement, and state accountability systems that reward readiness in both sectors. The K-12 and postsecondary systems must work together to integrate these various factors in order to move forward.

Figure 22 from *Beyond the Rhetoric* shows recommendations for a state college readiness agenda. The authors offer this recommended agenda as a

	10%	Highly selective institutions require high school diploma + college-prep curriculum + high grade-point average + high test scores + extras	Readiness Gap	Selective 4-year
Public Postsecondary Enrollments	30%	Less selective institutions require high school diploma + college-prep curriculum + usually a combination of grade-point average and/or test scores (but lower than most selective institutions)	Readiness Gap	Less selective 4-year
	60%	Non-selective (open-access) institutions require a high school diploma	Readiness Gap	Non-selective 2-year
	0% ———————— Percentage of students college ready ————→ 100%			

Figure 21: The Readiness Gap by Institutional Sector (Shulock et al. 2010, 2).
Reprinted with permission.

complement to what states are already doing in terms of initiatives aimed at alleviating readiness gaps.

Figure 23 is a checklist for moving the college readiness agenda forward. It is aimed at state governors, legislatures, K-12 school boards, postsecondary governing boards, and postsecondary coordinating boards.

In an ideal world, high school would thoroughly prepare students to do college-level work. Certainly, as a nation, we can foster reforms that will move us toward that ideal (and in the process, save money that goes towards remediation in college). The *Beyond the Rhetoric* issues brief is a valuable resource for state leaders both in government and in education.

Provide Effective Remediation/
Development Programs in College

Realistically, though, there will still be underprepared college students who have not benefitted from rigorous academic preparation.

So what do we do? Colleges and universities must have remediation programs in place that are effective at getting students from where they were when they entered to where they need to be. Colleges must have accurate assessments of students' levels of preparedness, particularly in Eng-

Instrument of change:	State policy
Target audience:	Governors, legislator, state education officials
Institutional focus:	P-12 and broad-access postsecondary institutions
Target population:	High school graduates eligible but not ready for postsecondary education
Readiness for what?	Two- and four-year degree programs, including career-oriented programs
Focus on standards:	Reading, writing, and mathematics
Meaning of "readiness":	Academic aspects of readiness only
Validation of standards:	Alignment of high school testing with postsecondary placement tests and introductory college courses
College-ready benchmark:	Success in introductory college-level courses

Figure 22: The Scope of the Recommended State College Readiness Agenda (Shulock et al. 2010, 10). Reprinted with permission.

lish and in mathematics, so that students are appropriately placed in courses they can manage successfully.

These programs must be sensitive to many students' feelings of frustration and demoralization because of being placed in developmental courses. Among two-year college students, developmental courses place an extra burden on them for tuition costs—61% of community college students take at least one remediation course (Adelman 2006).

In advising students who were placed in developmental courses, I would share with them that they were not alone. I'd tell them a majority of their peers needed some help to prepare them to do college-level work, and that these courses would help pave the way for their success in college.

One of my colleagues, who has taught all levels of math, gives students in his developmental math courses extra pep talks and extra tutoring. He tells his students how important it is for them to pass the developmental courses on their first try so they can save the money that repeating the course would entail and move on academically. He encourages them to seek tutoring from him and from the college math learning center so they are prepared to advance.

Focus on the First Year of College

Engle and Tinto report that 60% of low-income, first-generation students who leave higher education before earning a degree do so after the first

TAKING RESPONSIBILITY FOR COLLEGE READINESS:
A CHECKLIST

GOVERNORS SHOULD:

✔ Call for legislation that sets forth a framework for a comprehensive and systemic college readiness agenda

✔ Ensure that a P–16 council (if one exists) is charged to develop and advocate for a comprehensive and systemic college readiness agenda

✔ Communicate often and clearly about the importance of setting college readiness standards that truly signal readiness

✔ Set clear expectations that the broad-access postsecondary sectors (all two-year and less selective four-year institutions) work as equal partners on a college readiness agenda

✔ Ensure that readiness standards are adopted as a core component of state P–12 standards

LEGISLATURES SHOULD:

✔ Develop and pass legislation that sets forth a framework for a comprehensive and systemic college readiness agenda and assigns clear responsibility for its implementation

✔ Set clear expectations that the broad-access postsecondary sectors (all two-year and less selective four-year institutions)work as equal partners to establish and implement a college readiness agenda

✔ Revise accountability requirements to hold P–12 and postsecondary accountable for increasing the numbers of college-ready high school graduates

P–12 BOARDS SHOULD:

✔ Adopt, as a subset of content standards and in full partnership with postsecondary education, specific college readiness standards for reading, writing, and mathematics that set forth skills, knowledge, and performance levels that students need to succeed in entry-level college courses in two-year and four-year degree programs

✔ Adopt assessments that measure the acquisition of the specific skills and knowledge set forth in the adopted readiness standards

✔ Adopt changes to teacher preparation and teacher in-service to ensure that teachers are trained to help students reach the college readiness standards

✔ Oversee the development of curricular changes to improve college readiness, with a strong focus on new curriculum in 12th grade targeted to areas of identified need

POSTSECONDARY GOVERNING BOARDS SHOULD:

✔ Implement mechanisms for all broad-access postsecondary institutions to partner with P–12 education in the development of college readiness standards

✔ Adopt the college readiness standards officially

✔ Adopt one set of placement instruments and benchmarks across the broad-access sector that reflects the college readiness standards adopted by P–12 and postsecondary boards

POSTSECONDARY COORDINATING BOARDS SHOULD:

✔ Monitor the use of placement instruments and standards in use across the broad-access sector and work toward consistent use of placement regimens that reflect the state's college readiness standards

✔ Develop accountability metrics for monitoring changes in: the proportion of entering students who are college ready; the proportion of remedial students who transition to college-level studies; and the level of postsecondary access provided by these institutions

Figure 23: Taking Responsibility for College Readiness: A Checklist
(Shulock et al. 2010). Reprinted with permission.

year. In Engle and Tinto's words (2008, 28): "For too many low-income, first-generation students, the newly-opened door to American higher education has been a revolving one."

Engle and Tinto's report compiles recent research on the academic achievement gap and offers recommendations for educators and policymakers. Much of what follows is a distillation of their work.

Many colleges and universities have instituted "first-year seminar" courses, which seem to be effective at improving retention. The focus on the first year can take a variety of forms.

1. During the summer prior to entering college, offer orientation courses and continue them during the first year.

2. Create first-year learning communities.

3. Reach out to high-risk students early and often during the first year, encouraging them to get involved in college-related activities.

4. Offer what many colleges are calling "intrusive" advisement — making contact with advisors mandatory.

Remove Barriers to Success

Other research, reported by Engle and O'Brien (2007), shows that retention programs are most effective in reaching high-risk students when they are mandatory, when barriers that limit students' participation, such as cost, are removed, and when faculty or staff members are designated "first responders" to students' needs.

Engle and Tinto suggest (2008):

1. Monitoring student progress by developing early warning and/or advising systems with a high degree of communication between classroom faculty, staff in academic and social support systems, and students.

2. Offering study skills courses and tutoring programs and creating assurances that students who need them will use them.

3. Creating learning communities and other forms of supplemental instruction.

4. Offering developmental courses, such as writing, along with content courses.

5. Offering effective personal and career counseling and mentoring programs.

6. Providing special programs that target at-risk students and having "first-responders" staff readily available to them. Research shows that retention programs for the general student body may not improve at-risk student success; retention programs designed with the needs of at-risk students in mind, on the other hand, tend to be effective strategies that improve all students' chances for success.

Promote Student Engagement and Make Students the Heart of the Institution

With all the research supporting student engagement as a critical variable for student success, college leaders should ensure that professional faculty development on their campuses encourages faculty to use proven pedagogical strategies, such as those described in chapter 2, in their classes.

College leaders need to create a campus culture/climate that puts students at the heart of the institution and makes student success its reason for being.

Create a College-Going Culture in High Schools

In an issue brief, the National Governors Association (NGA) Center for Best Practices provides a kind of blueprint for how to create/implement a college-going culture in the secondary school system (2009, 8).

First, there should be a *college and career planning course* in secondary schools, so that postsecondary guidance reaches all students. Second, there should be *professional development for educators*. Third, there should be *student leadership training* so that students themselves spread a college-ready culture among the student body. Fourth, there should be a *college enrollment performance management system* so that school leaders can monitor whether their students are on the college path trajectory.

The NGA indicates that states need to improve students' readiness for college and careers. In addition to what has been said about providing rigorous high school courses, the governors note that high schools must have accurate assessments in place so students know whether they are prepared to do college-level work. High schools should also have programs of study that *integrate career and technical education with academic course work* and are linked to two-year degrees or certificates.

Teacher mentor programs, in which teachers supplement the work of high school counselors to help students make sound choices about the courses they need, have been quite successful, particularly for low-income, first-generation students (NGA 2009). NGA highlights College Summit, a national nonprofit organization working with urban and rural schools in twelve states, as a resource high schools can use for help in designing such teacher mentor programs. College Summit high schools raised their college enrollment rates by 15% among low-income, first-generation students, far surpassing the 4% national average for the same period of time.

Offer Support Programs for College Students

Bailey and Alfonso's research shows that the most effective support programs that states can fund are learning communities, especially at two-year colleges where students typically go to their classes and then leave campus. Learning communities can take many forms but the essential ingredients at the community college, non-residential level are that students go to classes as a cohort and instruction is organized around themes that overlap from class to class.

The NGA suggests that states look to public-private partnerships such as Year Up: Closing the Opportunity Divide, a program that attempts to recapture students who left college without earning a degree. Geared towards low-income students, Year Up provides postsecondary study, mentoring support, skills development, and job placement to get students back into college.

Promote College Success

What else can states do to promote academic college success? The NGA says that states must remove barriers that make it hard for two-year college students to transfer to four-year institutions. They recommend common course numbering and statewide articulation agreements among two-year and four-year institutions.

The NGA also suggests that states experiment with performance-based funding (2009). In other words, colleges and universities should be funded based on graduation rates rather than solely on enrollment rates. Colleges do need to be funded in part based on enrollment since they have to be able to support the students they admit. However, The NGA Issues Brief says that enrollment should not be the only consideration.

In fact, performance-based funding should be further refined. Moore and Shulock point out that funding should be based on milestones, that is, intermediate measures of student progress (2010). Several states have already adopted such an approach and many more are considering it.

Early performance-based funding dependent on graduation rates had some shortcomings: it failed to reward institutions for student progress. Moore and Shulock recommend a new funding model that includes financial incentives for colleges to get students to complete milestones—with extra incentives for milestones completed by underserved students (2010). The extra incentives would help close preparedness and income gaps.

States fail to create incentives for degree completion when funding is strictly enrollment-based and does not account for performance. Performance-based funding would make it more likely for colleges to pay attention to innovations and policies that improve completion rates. Examples of performance indicators and outcomes could include: successful completion of core courses, advancement from remedial to college-level courses, retention rates by semester or academic year, transfer rate from a two-year to a four-year institution, and of course, degree completion and total time to degree.

Give Underserved Students and their Parents What they Need for College Success

Other recommendations by Engle and Tinto involve giving low-income, first-generation students the kind of academic preparation they will need to gain access to college and to be successful once they get there (2008, 28). They say students and their parents need:

1. More information and counseling about gateway courses well before high school, especially since the math track to college starts with 8th grade algebra.

2. Additional academic and study skill support to successfully complete challenging high school coursework, including integrating note-taking, higher-order thinking, time management, and other academic self-advocacy skills into the core curriculum, given likely gaps in elementary and middle school preparation.

3. Greater access to college-preparatory courses, which are either not offered at the high schools they attend or are offered in watered-down formats that do not do much to prepare them to succeed in college, especially at four-year institutions.

4. Teachers who are equipped with the training and skills needed to develop challenging course material and teach rigorous college-preparatory courses, including Advanced Placement.

5. Counselors who have a more comprehensive knowledge of the college access process and the support and time they need to work with students on their pathway to college.

Engle and Tinto suggest targeting more financial aid to low-income, first-generation students so as to expand their options in their selection of schools. Most of this population attends community colleges because of cost factors. With more financial aid, they could either attend community college full-time or start college at a four-year institution—either of these possibilities would increase their chances of earning a degree.

Engle and Tinto suggest (2008, 28):

1. Workshops designed specifically for students—and their parents and guardians—about the financial aid process, especially filling out the FAFSA (Free Application for Federal Student Aid).

2. Additional information to improve their financial literacy about their options for paying the costs of attendance at four-year institutions, including the prudent use of loans. This includes how to budget and use the banking system, the pros and cons of credit card use, and other forms of financial literacy to help students better acquire and utilize their financial aid.

3. Increases in grant aid from institutional, state, and federal sources, which will require a shift away from merit aid at the institutional and state levels.

4. Greater assistance with covering "remaining" or unmet financial need, such as through the use of expanded work-study programs.

Engle and Tinto tell us that more than 60% of this demographic starts at two-year institutions and has aspirations to transfer and earn a bachelor's degree (2008, 28). Less than 5% actually do earn a B.A. To facilitate the transfer process from community college to a four-year institution, low-income, first-generation students need (Engle and Tinto 2008):

1. A clear vision of the long-term pathway from high school to a two-year college and a four-year college, with guidance from high school teachers and counselors during the college planning and choice process.

2. Effective developmental courses, particularly in mathematics, to address shortcomings in their academic preparation.

3. Strong transfer counseling and planning from academic advisors as well as favorable articulation policies.

4. Adequate financial counseling and aid (e.g., transfer scholarships), as well as other academic and social support to ensure successful degree completion after the transition.

Engle and Tinto say it is critical to provide low-income, first-generation students with support to ease the transition to college. Their recommendations include:

1. Beginning as early as elementary and middle school, exposing students to college tours and college and career assessment tools to inspire their interest and knowledge about the college environment.

2. Early intervention through bridge and orientation programs that socialize students to the expectations of the academic environment; involving parents also helps them to understand the demands of academic life.

3. Advising, tutoring, and mentoring by faculty and peers that maintain needed support throughout the college years.

4. Participation in special programs for at-risk populations that "scale down" the college experience for low-income, first-generation students by providing them with personalized attention from staff and a place to connect with supportive peers who share common backgrounds and experiences.

In order to encourage greater college engagement among low-income, first-generation students, colleges and universities must remove the barriers that prevent them from doing so. These barriers are primarily financial.

Engle and Tinto (2008, 29) suggest that colleges need to:

- Offer additional opportunities for work-study to increase the amount of time these students spend on campus while meeting their financial needs.
- Focus on increasing interaction and engagement in the classroom in order to make use of the only time many low-income, first-generation students spend on campus.
- Develop cohorts of study groups that foster campus community and provide an academic and social support system for low-income, first generation students.

Recruit Adults beyond Traditional College Age

A Lumina Foundation study indicates that most states can't meet the education target needs for the nation without including adults beyond the traditional college-going age (Pusser et al. 2007). The United States must get people who have opted out of the educational system back on the college track. Many people who leave the educational track come from low-income, first-generation backgrounds.

The following strategies for reengaging this demographic are offered by Engle and Tinto (2008, 29):

1. Provide support through programs that help adults complete their General Equivalency Diploma, like the Federal TRIO Educational Opportunity Centers.

2. Offer college credit for experiential learning in the workplace to expedite degree completion.

3. Develop programs to reach out to and serve students who leave college with a limited number of credits remaining to graduation like the program offered by the Oklahoma State Regents for Higher Education.

4. Expand financial aid eligibility for part-time students and/or provide additional resources (e.g. childcare) to promote persistence.

Increase Associate's Degree and Certificate Completers

As mentioned in chapter 1, other countries are passing us by in terms of two-year degree and certificate completers. The *Measuring Up 2008* report predicts that a shortfall of skilled workers will be largely attributable to our not graduating enough associate's degree earners or certificate completers (NCPPHE 2008a).

The fastest job growth will take place in occupations that require an associate's degree or postsecondary vocational certificate (Obama 2009). Without factoring in financial aid, the average tuition and fees at community colleges is typically less than half of what's demanded at public four-year colleges, and ten percent of what's demanded at private four-year colleges and universities (NCES 2006-2007).

Starting at a community college reduces students' overall tuition for a bachelor's degree. The trouble is that although community colleges enroll almost half our nation's college students, too few of them make it to the B.A. degree. Half of them never make it to the second year and only 30% of first-time students earn the A.A. degree within three years of enrolling.

As noted earlier, low-income, first-generation students are much more likely to attend two-year institutions than four-year colleges and universities.

President Obama, being aware of these trends, recently set a goal for America: to lead the world in higher education by 2020, mainly by increasing our number of certificate holders and community college graduates. To reach this goal, the federal government has strengthened Pell Grants, simplified the application for financial aid, and created competitive grants to improve and expand proven reforms.

The administration's bundle of programs is known as *The American Graduation Initiative: Stronger American Skills through Community Colleges* and was introduced July 14, 2009. It states that jobs requiring at least an associate's degree are projected to grow twice as fast as those requiring no college experience. The plan to reform our nation's community colleges calls for an additional five million community college graduates by 2020. President Obama described new initiatives to increase the effectiveness and impact of community colleges, raise graduation rates, modernize facilities, and create new online learning opportunities. He said, "These steps—an unprecedented increase in the support for community colleges—will help rebuild the capacity and competitiveness of America's workforce" (Obama 2009).

The American Graduation Initiative recognizes that:

Community colleges are the largest part of our higher education system, enrolling more than 6 million students, and growing rapidly. They feature affordable tuition, open admission policies, flexible course schedules, and convenient locations, and they are particularly important for students who are older, working, need remedial classes, or can only take classes part-time. They are also capable of working with businesses, industry, and government to create tailored training programs to meet economic needs such as nursing, health information technology, advanced manufacturing, and green jobs, and of providing customized training at the worksite. (Obama 2009)

Since community colleges are where the great majority of low-income, first-generation, and minority students enroll, this initiative seems to be right on target. Community college graduation rates and transfer rates must improve to close gaps among groups of students and to meet targets set for America's international standing.

In a similar vein, Achieving the Dream (an initiative funded by the Lumina Foundation) has been active since 2004. It works on many fronts and with numerous partners, chief among them Jobs for the Future (JFF). It emphasizes the use of data to drive change and works on the multiple fronts of campus life and research, public engagement, and public policy. Seven national partner organizations work with the Lumina Foundation to guide Achieving the Dream.

Achieving the Dream partners with states to (JFF 2010, 1):

1. Improve the collection and use of student outcome data to guide policy and institutional change; and

2. Help states implement a coherent policy set that removes obstacles to—and creates incentives for—improved student persistence and completion.

In *Good Data. Strong Commitment. Better Policy. Improved Outcomes* (JFF 2010), the authors explain how at their inception, most states focused on access to community colleges. Achieving the Dream shifted the focus to student success (completion) in community colleges, especially for low-income and underprepared students.

Achieving the Dream's lead partner, Jobs for the Future, teams up with participating states and sets forth a policy framework that guides state-level planning and decision making. This framework emphasizes (JFF 2010, 1):

1. A clear public policy commitment to student success;

2. A strong performance measurement and data-driven account-ability system;

3. Assessment and placement policies that accelerate the progress of underprepared students;

4. Incentives to promote student persistence and completion;

5. Aligned expectations and transitions across educational sec-tors.

States that work with Achieving the Dream have used this framework to create detailed action plans. These states and their community colleges have made policy changes and adjustments to institutional practice that have the potential to dramatically improve persistence and degree comple-tion for community college students.

Improve Graduation Rates for Hispanic Students

Improving college graduation rates for Hispanic students is particularly important given demographic shifts in America. Debra Santiago, co-author of *Taking Stock: Higher Education and Latinos* (2009), had this to say at the briefing and panel discussion held on Latino student success at the U.S. Visitor Center:

> President Obama's degree-completion goals are unattainable without improving Latino success...We are not a population on the margin – we're a significant part of this country and the coun-try's future depends on the ability of our educational system to accept this reality. (Santiago 2009)

Santiago also wrote, "The majority of Latino graduates are a product of completion by chance, not completion by design...Often, students are told they are the ones who have to change, when in fact the colleges them-selves need to adapt as well" (Santiago 2009).

Taking Stock: Higher Education and Latinos (Santiago 2009), which we mentioned in chapter 1, describes institutional practices proven to increase Latino student success. It is worth noting here that these practices have im-proved *all* students' success rates:

1. Creating learning communities

2. Providing supplemental instruction (e.g., learning and tutoring centers)

3. Identifying and restructuring "gatekeeper" courses, those courses that historically have kept students from moving on to other college courses

4. Proactively targeting Latino and other nontraditional students to utilize academic and support services offered by the college

Given the swell of Latinos in America, and the predictions for future growth of this group, and given their poor degree completion rates, this is a demographic that needs special attention. Swail et al. published a series of three reports on Latino students in the educational pipeline (2005). The purpose of the series is to provide a sense of the challenges facing Latino youth compared to White youth on their way to postsecondary education and the B.A. degree.

The series relies on data from the National Educational Longitudinal Study (NELS), sponsored by the National Center for Education Statistics in 1988 to follow 8th grade students from middle school through to the workforce. In total, over 26,000 8th grade students were surveyed in 1988, with follow-up surveys in 1990 (10th grade), 1992 (12th grade), 1994 (2 years after scheduled high school graduation), and finally in 2000 (8 years after scheduled high school graduation).

NELS gives us the clearest picture of students in and beyond the educational pipeline in America. It provides a glimpse of our nation's future through a look at the past experiences of the NELS cohort. It notes:

> Less than one quarter (23.2%) of Latino postsecondary students graduate with a four-year degree within 10 years of leaving high school—less than half the rate of White students (47.3%). But by taking into consideration student and family characteristics, postsecondary aspirations and planning behaviors, secondary school activities, postsecondary activities, and financial support factors, this study shows that the BA degree persistence gap between Latino and White students can be dramatically reduced by taking action in specific areas. (Swail et al. 2005, 1)

The results of this analysis are consistent with previous research on Latino students: socioeconomic status, parental expectations, planning, course-taking patterns, and student postsecondary behaviors all have a significant impact on degree completion.

The results also point to clear directions for further research and policy decisions: the factors with the most impact—planning and postsecondary behavior—produce changes greater than 40%, and in some cases 60%, in the probability of earning a B.A. degree.

Here are the report's findings (Swail et al. 2005, 2):

Family and Student Characteristics:

Latina students are 20% more likely to complete a four-year degree than their male counterparts. Middle-income Latino students had a 17% higher probability of completing a four-year degree than low-income Latino students.

Expectations and Aspirations:

Expecting their children to attend some college or to get a bachelor's degree had no significant effect for Latinos, but parental expectation of advanced degrees had a large and significant effect for Latinos, demonstrated by an increase in the probability of earning a B.A. by 46%.

Latino students planning for some college increased the probability of B.A. completion by 48%, and those who planned for a bachelor's degree increased the probability by 53%.

Preparation for Postsecondary Education:

Getting help in completing applications, applying for financial aid, and writing essays produced no significant effects for Latinos or Whites.

Course-taking patterns, however, did produce positive effects. Taking pre-calculus and calculus produced positive effects for both Whites and Latinos with increases of 20% and 12% respectively.

According to this analysis, remedial math served no one. However, remediation in English proved positive for Latinos with an increase of 26%.

Postsecondary Activities and Experiences:

Beginning postsecondary studies at a four-year institution increased the probability of completion by 29% and 35% for Latinos and Whites respectively.

Maintaining continuous enrollment increased the probability by 60% and 42% respectively.

Earning a GPA between 2.50 and 3.19 increased the probability of completion by 47% for Latinos and 42% for Whites and earning a GPA between 3.20 and 4.00 increased the probability of completion by 62% for Latinos and 45% for Whites.

Choosing to delay enrollment between high school and college reduced the probability of completion for Latinos by 20%.

Financial Aid:

This study showed there was no difference in the effect of receiving grants, loans, or participating in work study programs. However, this seems contradictory to much of the research, particularly the more recent research in *Measuring Up 2008* and the PEW Hispanic Reports by Mark Hugo Lopez and Richard Fry.

Postsecondary Planning and Academic Preparation:

The study found that preparation and planning need to begin in middle school.

Based on their findings regarding Latinos' successful degree completion, Swail et al. offer the following suggestions for policy making at three levels of education: middle school, high school, and postsecondary institutions (2005, 3). In their words:

Middle School:

The middle school level is critical according to our findings because Latinos who enter high school with a plan for any type of postsecondary study—with a sense of the purpose of their high school work—are far more likely to graduate college than those who have no plan. In fact, Latino students who had a plan to attend college improved the chances of graduation by 48% compared to other students. Of course, having a plan to attain a BA degree improves the chances by an additional 5% (53%).

Thus, developing college knowledge among students and families can have a major impact on future educational opportunities.

High School:

Academic preparation for college must begin immediately with the first math courses that students take. Latinos need to be enrolled in and master Algebra I no later than the ninth grade in order to reap the benefits of high mathematics achievement on postsecondary persistence. Latinos who take more than three years of mathematics beginning with Algebra I have a higher probability of graduating from college than those who take fewer than three courses. In addition, remediation in English is also important for Latinos.

It is during high school that solid advising must take place about postsecondary education and the type of institutions students and families should consider. Latinos seeking a four-year degree are somewhat disserved by beginning at a two-year institution.

Postsecondary Institution:

Helping Latinos maintain continuous enrollment and providing academic support while they are enrolled is the primary role of the postsecondary institution in the effort to improve the completion rates of Latinos. The provision of academic support is evinced as important by the large effect of grade point average on the probability of completion. Of course, being academically prepared when they enter is important for all students, but being able to take advantage of academic support services undoubtedly helps students to maintain high performance in an academic culture that differs significantly from high school.

Latino students who are supported by their families in the pursuit of a postsecondary education, create a plan by the eighth grade, take three years of mathematics or more, start at a four-year institution, and maintain continuous enrollment and a GPA of 2.50 or above can close the gap between Latinos and Whites in the completion of four-year degrees. The findings in this study do not suggest it will be easy to make these things a reality, but they do suggest where to begin.

In Conclusion

I hope the data provided in this book clearly lays out the challenge our nation faces: to educate more of its citizens and to concurrently narrow the gaps among diverse groups of students. Meeting this challenge will require a multifaceted approach that involves federal, state, and local governments; teaching faculty at all levels of education; and education administrative leaders. The educators and researchers cited in this book offer valuable suggestions for moving America forward.

Tool Box

In addition to the references at the end of this book, you may find the following references helpful. They were compiled by the National Conference of State Legislatures (NCSL 2008) for their article *Improving High Schools through Rigor, Relevance and Relationships*:

Clifford Adelman. 1999. *Answers in the Tool Box: Academic Intensity, Attendance Patterns, and Bachelor's Degree Attainment.* Washington, D.C.: U.S. Department of Education Office of Educational Research and Improvement.

Peter D. Hart Research Associates/Public Opinion Strategies. 2005. *Rising to the Challenge: Are High School Graduates Prepared for College and Work? A Study of Recent High School Graduates, College Instructors, and Employers.* Washington, D.C.: Achieve Inc.

The Education Trust–West. 2004. *The A-G Curriculum: College-Prep? Work-Prep? Life-Prep — Understanding and Implementing a Rigorous Core Curriculum for All.* Oakland, California: The Education Trust–West.

Clifford Adelman. 2004. *Principal Indicators of Student Academic Histories in Postsecondary Education, 1972-2000.* Washington, D.C.: U.S. Department of Education, Institute of Education Sciences.

Anthony P. Carnevale and Donna M. Desrochers. 2002. *Connecting Education Standards and Employment: Course-taking Patterns of Young Workers.* Washington, D.C.: Achieve Inc.

James J. Kemple and Judith Scott-Clayton. 2004. *Career Academies: Impacts on Labor Market Outcomes and Educational Attainment.* New York, New York: MDRC.

Thomas R. Bailey, Katherine L. Hughes, and Melinda Mechur Karp. 2002. *What Role Can Dual Enrollment Programs Play in Easing the Transition Between High School and Postsecondary Education?* New York, New York: Columbia University.

References

Adelman, Clifford. 2006. *The toolbox revisited: Paths to degree completion from high school through college*. Washington, DC: U.S. Department of Education.

Alliance for Children and Families. n.d. Demographics/Populations: Generations. *Alliance trends: Scanning the horizons*. Available online at: http://www.alliancetrends.org/demographics-population.cfm?id=34.

Allport, Gordon. 1954. *The nature of prejudice*. Reading, MA: Addison-Wesley.

American College Personnel Association. 1996. *The student learning imperative: Implications for student affairs*. Washington, DC: American College Personnel Association.

Anderson, L., et al 2005-2006. *Learner-centered teaching and education at USC: A resource for faculty*, Committee on Academic Programs and Teaching (CAPT), Learner Centered Task Force, University of Southern California.

Angelo, Thomas A. 1997. The campus as learning community: Seven promising shifts and seven powerful levers. *AAHE Bulletin*, 4 (9):3–6.

Angelo, Thomas A., and Kathryn Patricia Cross. 1993. *Classroom assessment techniques: A handbook for college teachers*. 2nd ed. San Francisco, CA: Jossey-Bass.

Aronson, Elliot, Nancy Blaney, Cookie Stephan, Jev Sikes, and Matthew Snapp. 1978. *The jigsaw classroom*. Beverly Hills, CA: Sage Publishing.

Association of American Colleges and Universities. 2002. *Greater expectations: A new vision for learning as a nation goes to college*. Washington, DC: Association of American Colleges and Universities.

Astin, Alexander W., Trudy W. Banta, Kathryn Patricia Cross, Elaine El-Khawas, Peter T. Ewell, Pat Hutchings, Theodore J. Marchese, Kay M. McClenney, Marcia Mentkowski, Margaret A. Miller, E. Thomas Moran, and Barbara D. Wright. 1997. Nine principles of good practice for assessing student learning. Available at: http://www.academicprograms.calpoly.edu/pdfs/assess/nine_principles_good_practice.pdf.

Aud, Susan, William Hussar, Michael Planty, Thomas Snyder, Kevin Bianco, Mary Ann Fox, Lauren Frohlich, Jana Kemp, and Lauren Drake. 2010. *The condition of education 2010* (NCES 2010-028). Washington, DC: The National Center for Education Statistics, Institute of Education Sciences, U.S. Department of Education.

Bailey, Thomas R., and Mariana Alfonso. 2005. *Paths to persistence: An analysis of research on program effectiveness at community colleges*. New York, NY: Community College Research Center, Teachers College, Columbia University.

Bain, Ken, and James Zimmerman. 2009. Understanding great teaching. *Association of American Colleges and Universities*, 11 (2).

Bain, Ken. 2004. *What the best college teachers do*. Cambridge, MA: Harvard University Press.

Bair, E. Scott. 2000. Developing analytical and communication skills in a mock-trial course based on the famous Woburn, Massachusetts case. *Journal of Geoscience Education*, 48 (4): 450–454.

Bank, Barbara J., Ricky L. Slavings, and Bruce J. Biddle. 1990. Effects of peer, faculty, and parental influences on student persistence. *The Sociological Quarterly*, 63: 208–225.

Barr, Robert B., and John Tagg. 1995. From teaching to learning: A new paradigm for undergraduate education. *Change*, 27 (6):13–25.

Baud, David. 1995. Assessment and learning: Contradictory or complimentary? In *Assessment for Learning in Higher Education*, edited by Peter Knight. London, England: Kogan Page.

Baum, Sandy, Jennifer Ma, and Kathleen Payea. 2010. *Education pays 2010: The benefits of higher education for individuals and society*. Report of the College Board Advisory and Policy Center, New York, NY. Available at: http://trends.collegeboard.org/files/Education_Pays_2010.pdf.

Blatner, Adam. 2002. *Role playing in education*. Available at http://www.blatner.com/adam/pdntbk/rlplayedu.htm

Bligh, Donald A. 2000. What's the use of lectures? San Francisco, CA: Jossey-Bass.

Bloom, Benjamin S. 1956. *Taxonomy of educational objectives. Handbook 1: The cognitive domain*. New York, NY: David McKay.

Blumberg, Phyllis. 2007. Problem-based learning: A prototypical example of learning-centered teaching. *Journal of Student Centered Learning*, 3 (2):111–125.

Blumberg, Phyllis. 2009. *Developing learner-centered teaching: A practical guide for faculty*. San Francisco, CA: Jossey-Bass.

Bonwell, Charles C., and James A. Eison. 1991. *Active learning: Creating excitement in the classroom*. ASHE–ERIC Higher Education Report No. 1. Washington, DC: The George Washington University, School of Education and Human Development.

Bowen, William G., Matthew M. Chingos, and Michael S. McPherson. 2009. *Getting to the finish line: Completing college at America's public universities*. Princeton, NJ: Princeton University Press.

Bransford, John D., Ann L. Brown, and Rodney R. Cocking, eds. 1999. *How people learn: Brain, mind, experience, and school*. Washington, D.C.: The National Academy Press.

Burns, M.U. 1999. All the world's a stage. *NEA Higher Education Advocate* 17: 5–8.

Carnegie Mellon University, Enhancing Education, n.d. Grading and performance rubrics. *Design & teach a course*. Available at: http://www.cmu.edu/teaching/designteach/teach/rubrics.html.

Carnegie Mellon University. n.d. *Whys and hows of assessment*. Available online at: www.cmu.edu/teaching/assessment/howto/basics/formative-summative.html.

Carnegie Mellon University. 2008. *Assessment task force 6-month report with general findings and preliminary conclusions*. Prepared by Susan Ambrose, Tarini Bedi, Anne Fay, and Brian Junker. Available at: http://www.cmu.edu/teaching/assessment/ATFdocs/atf1styear report.pdf.

Carnevale, Anthony P. 2009. College affordability: The wolf in sheep's clothing. *Inside Higher Ed*. Available at: http://www.insidehighered.com/views/2009/01/12/carnevale.

Carnevale, Anthony, Nicole Smith, and Jeff Strohl. 2010. *Help wanted: Projections of jobs and education requirements through 2018*. Washington, DC: Center on Education and the Worksforce, Georgetown University.

Center for Community College Student Engagement (CCCSE). 2009. *Making connections: Dimensions of student engagement (2009 CCSSE Findings)*. Austin, TX: The University of Texas at Austin, Community College Leadership Program. Available at: http://www. ccsse.org/publications/national_report_2009/CCSSE09_execsum.pdf.

Cleveland State University Center for Teaching and Learning. n.d. *Active learning for almost any size class*. Available at: http://www.csuohio.edu/uctl/tips/tchtips3.2.html.

College Success Foundation. 2010. *Unleashing America's potential: The college success foundation 10th anniversary report. A proven model of success inspiring low-income, underserved youth to graduate high school and complete a college degree*. Issaquah, WA: College Success Foundation. Available at: http://www.collegesuccessfoundation.org/Document.Doc?id=24.

Chen, Xianglei. 2005. *First-generation students in postsecondary education: A look at their college transcripts*. Washington, DC: National Center for Education Statistics.

Chickering, Arthur, and Zelda F. Gamson. 1987. Seven principles for good practice. *AAHE Bulletin*, 39: 3–7.

Choy, Susan. 2000. *Low-income students: Who they are and how they pay for their education*. Washington, DC: National Center for Education Statistics.

Choy, Susan. 2001. *Students whose parents did not go to college: Postsecondary access, persistence, and attainment*. Washington, DC: National Center For Education Statistics.

Christensen, C. Roland. 1982. Foreword. In *The art and craft of teaching*, edited by Margaret M. Gullette. Cambridge, MA: Harvard University Danforth Center for Teaching and Learning.

Clement, Mary. 2009. Ten ways to engage your students on the first day of class. Recording of online seminar originally broadcast June 24. Madison, WI: Magna Publications.

Crone, Ian, and Kathy MacKay. 2007. Motivating today's college students. *Peer Review*, 9 (1):18–21.

Cummings, Jim. 2001. Empowering minority students: A framework for intervention. *Harvard Educational Review*, 71 (4).656–676.

Dallimore, Elise J., Julie H. Hertenstein, and Margorie B. Platt. 2004. Faculty-generated strategies for "cold calling" use: A comparative analysis with student recommendations. Journal on Excellence in College Teaching, 16 (1):23–62.

Davies, Mary Ann, and Michael Wavering. 1999. Alternative assessment: New directions in teaching and learning. *Contemporary Education*, 71 (1):39–45.

DeLong, Matt, and Dale Winter. 2002. *Learning to teach and teaching to learn mathematics: Resources for professional development*. Washington, DC: Mathematical Association of America.

Dewey, John. 1963. *Experience and education*. New York, NY: Collier Books.

Downing, Skip. 2010. *On course: Strategies for creating success in college and in life*. 6th ed. Florence, KY: Wadsworth/Cengage.

Doyle, Terry. 2008. The learner-centered classroom: A clear rationale for learner-centered teaching. *Learner Centered Teaching*. Available at: http://learnercenteredteaching.word press.com/articles-and-books/the-learner-centered-classroom/.

Editorial Projects in Education. 2009. Diplomas count. Broader horizons: The challenge of college readiness for all students. *Education Week*, 28 (34).

The Education Trust. 2010a. *Big gaps, small gaps: Some colleges and universities do better than others in graduating African-American students*. Washington, DC: The Education Trust.

The Education Trust. 2010b. *Big gaps, small gaps: Some colleges and universities do better than others in graduating Hispanic students*. Washington, DC: The Education Trust.

Educational Broadcasting Corporation. 2004. *Workshop: Cooperative and collaborative learning*. Available at: http://thirteen.org/edonline/concept2class/coopcollab/index.html.

Engle, Jennifer, and Colleen O'Brien. 2007. *Demography is not destiny: Increasing the graduation rates of low-income college students at large public universities*. Washington, DC: Pell Institute for the Study of Opportunity in Higher Education.

Engle, Jennifer, and Christina Theokas. 2010. *Top gap closers. Some public four-year colleges and universities have made good progress in closing graduation-rate gaps*. College Results Online. Washington, DC: The Education Trust.

Engle, Jennifer, and Vincent Tinto. 2008. *Moving beyond access: College success for low-income, first generation students*. Washington, DC: Pell Institute for the Study of Opportunity in Higher Education. Available at: http://www.coenet.us/files/files-Moving_Beyond_Access_2008.pdf.

Engstrom, Cathy M., and Vincent Tinto. 2008. Learning better together: The impact of learning communities on the persistence of low-income students. *Opportunity MATTERS*, 1: 5–21.

Fassinger, Polly A. 1996. Professors' and students' perception of why students participate in class. *Teaching Sociology*, 24 (1):25–33.

Felder, Richard M., Gary Felder, and E. Jacquelin Dietz. 1998. A longitudinal study of engineering student performance and retention vs. comparisons with traditionally-taught students. *Journal of Engineering Education*, 87 (4):469–480.

Freire, Paulo. 1970. *Pedagogy of the oppressed*. New York, NY: Herder and Herder.

Freeman, Tierra M., Lynley Anderman, and Jane M. Jensen. 2007. Sense of belonging in college freshman at the classroom and campus levels. *The Journal of Experimental Education*, 75 (3):203–220.

Frost, Winston L. 1999. It takes a community to retain a student: The Trinity Law School model. *Journal of College Student Retention: Research, Theory, and Practice*, 1 (3):203–224.

Fry, Richard. 2009. *The changing pathways of Hispanic youths into adulthood*. Washington, DC: The Pew Hispanic Center. Available at: http://pewhispanic.org/files/reports/114.pdf.

Goldschmid, Marcel L. 1971. The learning cell: An instructional innovation. *Learning and Development*, 2 (5):1–6.

Goldschmid, Marcel L. 1975. When students teach students. Paper presented at the International Conference on Improving University Teaching, Heidelberg, Germany.

Goldschmid, Marcel L., and Bruce M. Shore. 1974. The learning cell: A field test of an educational innovation. In *Methodological problems in research and development in higher education*, edited by W.A. Verreck. Amsterdam, The Netherlands: Swets and Zeitlinger.

Haffie, Tom. 2010. Broadcollecting: Using personal response systems ("clickers") to transform classroom interaction. In *The Dynamic Classroom: Engaging Students in Higher Education*, edited by Catherine Black, 135-146. Madison, WI: Atwood Publishing.

Hake, Richard R. 1997. Interactive-engagement vs. traditional methods: A six-thousand-student survey of mechanics test data for introductory physics courses. *American Journal of Physics*, 66: 64–74.

Harris, Michale, Roxanne Cullen, and Maryellen Weimer. 2010. *Leading the learner-centered classroom: An administrator's framework for improving student learning outcomes*. San Francisco, CA: Jossey-Bass.

Horn, Laura, and Anne-Marie Nuñez. 2000. *Mapping the road to college: First-generation students' math track, planning strategies, and context of support*. Washington, DC: National Center for Education Statistics.

Huba, Mary E., and Jann E. Freed. 2000. *Learner-centered assessment on college campuses: Shifting the focus from teaching to learning*. Boston, MA: Allyn & Bacon.

Jairam, Dharmananda, and Kenneth Kiewra. 2010. Helping students soar to success on computers: An investigation of the SOAR study method for computer-based learning. *The Journal of Educational Psychology*, 102 (3):601–614.

Jobs for the Future (JFF). 2010. *Good data. Strong commitment. Better policy. Improved outcomes*. Boston, MA: JFF. Available at: http://www.jff.org/publications/education/good-data-strong-commitment-better-polic.1046.

Johnson, David W., Roger T. Johnson, and Karl A. Smith. 1991. *Cooperative learning: Increasing college faculty instructional productivity*. ASHE–ERIC Higher Education Report No. 4. Washington, DC: The George Washington University, School of Education and Human Development.

Johnson, David W., Roger T. Johnson, and Karl A. Smith. 1998. Cooperative learning returns to college: What evidence is there that it works? *Change*, 30 (4):26–35. Available at: http://www.ce.umn.edu/~smith/docs/CLReturnstoCollege.pdf

Johnson, Jean, and Jon Rochkind, with Amber N. Ott and Samantha DuPont. 2009. *With their whole lives ahead of them: Myths and realities about why so many students fail to finish college*. New York, NY: Public Agenda.

Jungst, Steven E., Barbara L. Licklider, and Janice A. Wiersema. 2003. Providing support for faculty who wish to shift to a learning-centered paradigm in their higher education classrooms. *Journal of Scholarship of Teaching and Learning*, 3 (3):69-81.

Kennesaw State University Educational Technology Center. n.d. Assessment rubrics. Available online at: http://edtech.kennesaw.edu/intech/rubrics.htm.

King, Alison. 1990. Enhancing peer interaction and learning in the classroom. *American Educational Research Journal*, 27: 664–687.

Kraemer, Barbara A. 1997. The academic and social integration of Hispanic students into college. *Review of Higher Education*, 20 (2):163–179.

Kuh, George D., Ty M. Cruce, Rick Shoup, Jillian Kinzie, and Robert M. Gonyea. 2008. Unmasking the effects of student engagement on first-year college grades and persistence. *Journal of Higher Education*, 79 (5):540–563.

Kuh, George D., Jillian Kinzie, Ty M. Cruce, Rick Shoup, and Robert M. Gonyea. 2007. *Connecting the dots: Multi-faceted analyses of the relationships between student engagement: Results from the NSSE, and the institutional practices and conditions that foster student success.* Bloomington, IN: Indiana University Center for Post Secondary Research.

Kuh, Geogre D., Jillian Kinzie, John H. Schuh, Elizabeth J. Whitt, and associates. 2005. *Student success in college: Creating conditions that matter.* San Francisco, CA: Jossey-Bass.

Larrabee, Amy, and Erica Robinson. 2001. *Ready or not, here they come: Motivating and retaining the millennial generation.* Atlanta, GA: Bell Oaks Executive Research.

Lerner, Jennifer Brown, and Betsy Brand. 2006. *The college ladder: Linking secondary and postsecondary education for success for all students.* Washington, DC: American Youth Policy Forum.

Lewin, Tamar. 2008. Higher education may soon be unaffordable for most Americans, report says. *The New York Times*, Dec. 3.

Lopez, Mark Hugo. 2009. *Latinos and education: Explaining the attainment gap.* Washington, DC: Pew Hispanic Center. Available at: http://pewhispanic.org/files/reports/115.pdf.

Lumina Foundation for Education. 2009. *A stronger nation through education: How and why Americans must meet a "big goal" for college attainment.* Indianapolis, IN: Lumina Foundation for Education.

Magnan, Robert. *147 Practical tips for using icebreakers with college students.* 2005. Madison, WI: Atwood Publishing.

Marklein, Mary Beth. 2008. The world is moving past USA in higher ed. *USA Today*, December 3.

McCombs, Barbara L. 1997. Self-assessment and reflection: Tools for promoting teacher changes toward learner-centered practices. *NASSP Bulletin*, 81 (587):1–14.

McCombs, Barbara L. 1999. *The assessment of learner-centered practices (ALCP): Tools for teacher reflection , learning, and change.* Denver, CO: University of Denver Research Institute.

McCombs, Barbara L., and Lynda Miller. 2007. *Learner-centered classroom practices and assessments: Maximizing student motivation and achievement.* Thousand Oaks, CA: Corwin Press.

McDaniel, E. 1994. *Understanding education assessment.* Madison, WI: WCB Brown & Benchmark.

McGlynn, Angela P. 2001. *Successful beginnings for college teaching: Engaging your students from the first day.* Madison, WI: Atwood Publishing.

McGlynn, Angela P. 2007a. *Teaching today's college students: Widening the circle of success.* Madison, WI: Atwood Publishing.

McGlynn, Angela P. 2007b. More women than men in college: Equity implications for admissions. *The Hispanic Outlook in Higher Education*, 18 (3):16–17.

McGlynn, Angela P. 2007c. Student engagement: Especially good for the underprepared. *The Hispanic Outlook in Higher Education*, 17 (8):28–29.

McGlynn, Angela P. 2007d. NCES Releases Report on Educating Racial and Ethnic Minorities, *The Hispanic Outlook in Higher Education*,18 (15):26-27.

McGlynn, Angela P. 2008a. Expanding the college track for access and success. *The Hispanic Outlook in Higher Education*, 18 (16):20–21.

McGlynn, Angela P. 2008b. Report describes proven pathways to success for minority students. *The Hispanic Outlook in Higher Education*, 18 (24):24–27.

McGlynn, Angela P. 2009a. The condition of Latinos in education: Excelencia looks at the data. *The Hispanic Outlook in Higher Education*, 19 (14):19–21.

McGlynn, Angela P. 2009b. The plight of higher education: Affordability, barriers, completion rates. *The Hispanic Outlook in Higher Education*, 19 (14):32–33.

McGlynn, Angela P. 2010. Kaiser study shows media use by youth is heavy and rising, *The Hispanic Outlook in Higher Education*. 20 (19):26-28.

McKeachie, Wilbert J., and Marilla Svinicki. 2006. *McKeachie's teaching tips: Strategies, research, and theory for college and university teaching*. 12th ed. Wadsworth/Cengage.

McKeachie, Wilbert J., and Marilla Svinicki. 2011. *McKeachie's teaching tips: Strategies, research, and theory for college and university teaching*. 13th ed. Wadsworth/Cengage.

McKeachie, W.J., Paul R. Pintrich, Yi-Guang Lin, and David A. F. Smith. 1986. *Teaching and learning in the college classroom: A review of the research literature*. Ann Arbor, MI: The Regents of the University of Michigan.

Mezeske, Barbara. 2004. Shifting paradigms? Don't forget to tell your students. *The Teaching Professor*, 18 (7):1.

Milton, Ohmer, Howard R. Pollio, and James A. Eison. 1986. *Making sense of college grades*. San Francisco, CA: Jossey-Bass.

Moore, Colleen, and Nancy Shulock. 2010. *Divided we fail: Improving completion and closing racial gaps in california's community colleges*. Sacramento, CA: Institute for Education Leadership and Policy, California State University–Sacramento.

Mortenson, Thomas. 2009. Family income and educational attainment 1970 to 2007. *Postsecondary education opportunity: Public policy analysis and opportunity for postsecondary education*. 209 (1–16). Available at: http://www.kentuckycan.org/postSecEducNov2009.pdf.

Mueller, Jonathan. F. n.d.*Authentic assessment toolbox: Rubrics*. Available at: http://jfmueller.faculty.noctrl.edu/toolbox/rubrics.htm.

Muirhead, Brent. 2002. Relevant assessment strategies for online colleges and universities. *USDLA Journal*, 16 (2).

National Center for Education Statistics (NCES). 2010. Digest of Education Statistics (NCES 2010-013). US Department of Education Institute of Education Statistics. Washington D.C. Available at: http://nces.ed.gov/programs/digest/d09/.

National Center for Public Policy and Higher Education (NCPPHE). 2008a. *Measuring up 2008. The national report card on higher education*. San Jose, CA: NCPPHE. Available at: http://measuringup2008.highereducation.org/print/NCPPHEMUNationalRpt.pdf.

National Center for Public Policy and Higher Education (NCPPHE). 2008b. Study flunks 49 states in college affordability. *Community College Week*, 21 (9):8.

National Center for Public Policy and Higher Education and The Southern Regional Educational Board. 2010. Shulock, N. et. al, *Beyond the rhetoric: Improving college readiness through coherent state policy*. San Jose, CA: National Center for Public Policy and Higher Education. Available at: http://www.highereducation.org/reports/college_readiness/CollegeReadiness.pdf.

National Conference on State Legislatures (NCSL). 2008. *Improving high schools through rigor, relevance, and relationships*. Washington, DC: NCSL. Available at: http://www.ncsl.org/default.aspx?tabid=12879.

National Council for Adult and Experiential Learning (CAEL) and Natonal Center for Higher Education Management Systems (NCHEMS). 2008. *Adult learning in focus*. Indianapolis, IN: Lumina Foundation for Education.

National Governors' Association Center for Best Practices (NGA). 2009. *Issue brief: Increasing college success: A road map for governors*. Available at:http://www.nga.org/Files/pdf/0912INCREASINGCOLLEGESUCCESS.PDF. Washington, DC: NGA.

National Leadership Council for Liberal Education and America's Promise. 2007. *College learning for the new global century*. Washington, DC: AAC&U.

National Survey of Student Engagement (NSSE). 2009. *Annual results 2009: Assessment for improvement: Tracking student engagement over time*. Bloomington, IN: NSSE. Available at: http://nsse.iub.edu/NSSE_2009_Results/.

National Survey of Student Engagement (NSSE). 2007. *Experiences that matter: Enhancing student learning and success*. Bloomington, IN: NSSE. Available at: http://nsse.iub.edu/NSSE_2007_Results/.

National Survey of Student Engagement (NSSE). 2006. *Engaged learning: Fostering success for all students*. Bloomington, IN: NSSE. Available at: http://nsse.iub.edu/NSSE_2006_Results/.

National Survey of Student Engagement (NSSE). 2005. *Exploring different dimensions of student engagment*. Bloomington, IN: NSSE. Available at: http://nsse.iub.edu/NSSE_2005_Results/.

Nilson, Linda B. 2010. Matching teaching methods with student learning outcomes. Presentation at the Southern Association of Colleges and Schools Summer Institute, Tampa, FL.

Nilson, Linda B. 2003. *Teaching at its best: A research-based resource for college instructors*. 2nd ed. San Francisco, CA: Anker Publishing Co.

Obama, President Barack, July 14, 2009. *Investing in Education: the American Graduation Initiative*, Remarks at Macomb Community College, Michigan. Available at: http://www.whitehouse.gov/the_press_office/Remarks-by-the-President-on-the-American-Graduation-Initiative-in-Warren-MI/

O'Banion, Terry. 2010. Focus on learning: The core mission of higher education. In *Focus on Learning: The Learning College Reader*, edited by Terry O'Banion and Cynthia Wilson (1–12). Phoenix, AZ: The League for Innovation in the Community College.

O'Brien, Judith Grunert, Barbara J. Millis, and Margaret W. Cohen. 2008. *The course syllabus: A learning-centered approach*. 2nd ed. San Francisco, CA: Jossey-Bass.

Oblinger, Diana. 2003. Boomers, gen-xers, and millennials: Understanding the new students. *EDUCAUSE Review*, 38 (4):37–47.

On Course. n.d. Student success strategies. Available online at: http://www.oncourseworkshop.com/Student%20Success%20Strategies.htm.

On Course. n.d. The case for learner-centered education. Available online at: http://www.oncourseworkshop.com/Miscellaneous018.htm.

Organization for Economic Co-operation and Development (OECD). 2010. *Education at a glance. OECD indicators*. Paris, France: OECD Publications.

Padilla, Raymond V. 1999. College student retention: Focus on success. *Journal of College Student Retention: Research, Theory, and Practice*, 1 (2):131–146.

Palmer, Parker J. 1998. *The courage to teach*. San Francisco, CA: Jossey Bass.

Pankratz, Roger, Sue McCullough, Barbara Chesler, Debra Frazier, James Becker, and Jamie Spugnardi. 2004. *The renaissance project for improving teacher quality: Classroom assessment tools that support high-performing teacher work samples*. Available at: http://www.emporia.edu/teach/tws/docs/renaissanceTwsSupport.htm.

Pascarella, Ernest T., and Patrick T. Terenzini. 1991. *How college affects students: Findings and insights from twenty years of research*. San Francisco, CA: Jossey-Bass.

Pascarella, Ernest T., and Patrick T. Terenzini. 2005. *How college affects students*. Volume 2, *A third decade of research*. San Francisco, CA: Jossey-Bass.

Paulson, Donald R., and Jennifer L. Faust. 2002. *Active learning for the classroom*. Online monograph available at: http://www.calstatela.edu/dept/chem/chem2/Active/index.htm.

Pell Institute. 2007. *Demography is not destiny: Increasing the graduation rates of low-income college students at large public universities*. Available at: http://www.pellinstitute.org/files/files-demography_is_not_destiny.pdf

Penner, Jon G. 1984. *Why many college teachers cannot lecture: How to avoid communication breakdown in the classroom*. Springfield, IL: Charles C. Thomas.

Pew Hispanic Center. 2008. *Statistical portrait of Hispanics in the United States, 2008*. Available at: http://pewhispanic.org/factsheets/factsheet.php?factsheetID=58.

Pew Research Center. 2010. *Millennials: A portrait of Generation Next. Confident. Connected. Open to change*. Washington, DC: Pew Research Center. Available at: http://pewsocialtrends.org/files/2010/10/pdf/millennials-confident-connected-open-to-change.pdf.

Piaget, Jean. 1952. *The origins of intelligence in children*. Translated by Margaret Cook. New York, NY: International Universities Press.

Planty, Michael, William Hussar, Thomas Snyder, Grace Kena, Angelina KewalRamani, Jana Kemp, Kevin Bianco, Rachel Dinkes. 2009. *The Condition of Education 2009*.

(NCES 2009-081). Washington, DC: National Center for Education Statistics, Institute of Education Sciences, U.S. Department of Education.

Prensky, Marc. 2001a. *Digital game-based learning*. New York, NY: McGraw-Hill.

Prensky, Marc. 2001b. Digital natives, digital immigrants. *On the Horizon*, 9 (5):1–6.

Pressley, Michael, Eileen Wood, Vera E. Woloshyn, Vicki Martin, Alison King, and Deborah Menke.1992. Encouraging mindful use of prior knowledge: Attempting to construct explanatory answers facilitates learning. *Educational Psychologist*, 27 (1):91–109.

Prince, Michael. 2004. Does active learning work? A review of the research. *Journal of Engineering Education*, 93 (3):223–232.

Pusser, Brian, David W. Breneman, Bruce M. Gansneder, Kay J. Kohl, John S. Levin, John H. Milam and Sarah E. Turner. 2007. Returning to learning: Adults' success in college is key to America's future. *Lumina Foundation, New Agenda Series*. Indianapolis, IN: Lumina Foundation for Education.

Ratey, John J. 2002. *A user's guide to the brain: Perception, attention, and the four theaters of the brain*. New York, NY: Vintage Books.

Richards, Alex. 2011. Census data show rise in college degrees, but also in racial gaps in education. *Chronicle of Higher Education*, Jan. 23, 2011. Available at: http://chronicle.com/section/Facts-Figures/58/.

Rideout, Victoria J., Ulla G. Foehr, and Donald F. Roberts. 2010. Generation M2: Media in the lives of 8- to 18-year-olds. *Kaiser Family Foundation Study*. Available online at: http://www.kff.org/entmedia/upload/8010.pdf.

Rochester Institute of Technology (RIT), Student Learning Outcomes Assessment Office. 2011. *Creating practical and meaningful course-level assessment of student learning*. Available at: http://www.rit.edu/academicaffairs/outcomes/media/documents/Course_Assessment_Guide_V2.pdf.

Rockwood, Horace S., III. 1995a. Cooperative and collaborative learning. *The National Teaching & Learning Forum*, 4 (6):8–9.

Rockwood, Horace S., III. 1995b. Cooperative and collaborative learning. *The National Teaching & Learning Forum*, 5 (1):8–10.

Roderick, Melissa, Jenny Nagaoka, Vanessa Coca, and Eliza Moeller, with Karen Roddie, Jamiliyah Gilliam, and Desmond Patton. 2008. *From high school to the future: Potholes on the road to college*. Chicago, IL: Consortium on Chicago School Research.

Rodgers, Ruth. 2010. What to teach when there isn't time to teach everything. Recording of online seminar originally broadcast August 26. Madison, WI: Magna Publications.

Santiago, Deborah A. 2008. *The condition of Latinos in education: 2008 Factbook*. Washington, DC: Excelencia in Education. Available at: http://www.edexcelencia.org/research/conditions-latinos-education-2008-factbook.

Santiago, Deborah A., and Travis Reindl. 2009. *Taking stock: Higher education and Latinos*. Washington, DC: Excelencia in Education. Available at : www.EdExcelencia.org/research/taking-stock-latinos-higher-education.

Shulock, Nancy, et al. 2010. *Beyond the rhetoric: Improving college readiness through coherent state policy*. San Jose, CA: National Center for Public Policy and Higher Education and The Southern Regional Educational Board. Available at: http://www.highereducation.org/reports/college_readiness/CollegeReadiness.pdf.

Silberman, Melvin L. 1996. *Active learning: 101 Strategies to teach any subject*. Needham Heights, MA: Allyn & Bacon.

Skiba, Diane J., and Amy J. Barton. 2006. Adapting your teaching to accommodate the Net generation of learners. *The Online Journal of Issues in Nursing*, 11 (2). Available at: http://www.nursingworld.org/MainMenuCategories/ANAMarketplace/ANAperiodicals/OJIN/TableofContents/Volume112006/No2May06/tpc30_416076.as.

Smetanka, Mary Jane. 2004. Millennial students: A new crew enlivens the "U." *The Minneapolis Star Tribune*, May 7, 1.A.

Smith, Gary A. 2008. First-day questions for the learner-centered classroom. *The National Teaching & Learning Forum*, 17 (5). Available at: http://www.ntlf.com/html/ti/V17n5comp.pdf.

Smith, Steve. 2010. Technology hasn't helped students' study skills, research finds. *Faculty Focus*. Madison, WI: Magna Publications.

Springer, Leonard, Mary Elizabeth Stanne, and Samuel Donovan. 1997. *Effects of cooperative learning on undergraduates in science, mathematics, engineering, and technology: A meta-analysis*. (Research Monograph No. 11). Madison, WI: University of Wisconsin-Madison, National Institute for Science.

Stark, Diane. *Professional development module on Active learning. Texas collaborative for teaching excellence*. Corpus Christi, TX: Del Mar College. Available at: http://www.texas collaborative.org/activelearning.htm

Steckol, Karen F. 2007. Learner-centered teaching in higher education: formative assessment study turns classroom into research lab. *The ASHA Leader*, 12 (5):14–15.

Swail, Watson Scott, Alberto F. Cabrera, Chul Lee, and Adriane Williams. 2005. *Latino students and the educational pipeline. A three-part series*. Part III: *Pathways to the bachelor's degree for Latino students*. Washington, DC: The Educational Policy Institute. Available at: http://www.educationalpolicy.org/pdf/LatinoIII.pdf.

Swail, Watson Scott, Kenneth E. Redd, and Laura W. Perna. 2003. Retaining minority students in higher education: A framework for success. *ASHE–ERIC Higher Education Report*, 30 (2). Available at: http://www.educationalpolicy.org/pdf/Swail_Retention_Book.pdf.

Taylor, Mark. 2010. Teaching generation neXt: A pedagogy for today's learners. In *A Collection of Papers on Self-Study and Institutional Improvement*. 26th ed. Chicago, IL: The Higher Learning Commission.

Taylor, Paul, and Scott Keeter, eds. 2010. *Millennials: A Portrait of generation next. Confident. Connected. Open to change*. Washington, DC: Pew Research Center. Available at: http://pewsocialtrends.org/assets/pdf/millennials-confident-connected-open-to-change.pdf.

Thompson, Janette, B. Licklider, and Steven E. Jungst. 2003. Learner-centered teaching: Postsecondary strategies that promote "thinking like a professional." *Theory in Practice*, 42 (2):133–141.

Timpson, William M. Silvia Sara Canetto, Evelinn A. Borrayo, and Raymond Yang. 2003. *Teaching diversity: Challenges and complexities, identities and integrity*. Madison, WI: Atwood Publishing.

Timpson, William M., Silvia Sara Canetto, Evelinn A. Borrayo, and Raymond Yang, eds. 2005. *147 Practical tips for teaching diversity*. Madison, WI: Atwood Publishing.

Tinto, Vincent. 1994. *Leaving college: Rethinking the causes of student attrition*. 2nd ed. Chicago, IL: University of Chicago Press.

Tinto, Vincent. 1998. Colleges as communities: Taking research on student persistence seriously. *The Review of Higher Education*, 21 (2):167–177.

Tinto, Vincent. 2003. Promoting student retention through classroom practice. Presented at Enhancing Student Retention: Using International Policy and Practice. An international conference sponsored by the European Access Network and the Institute for Access Studies at Staffordshire University in Amsterdam, Nov. 5–7.

Tomsho, Robert. 2008. For college-bound, new barriers to entry: Their budgets squeezed, state schools cap enrollment, weigh tuition increases; fears for low-income students. *The Wall Street Journal*. Dec. 3. Available at: http://online.wsj.com/article/SB122826544902474353.html.

UNESCO Institute for Statistics (UIS). 2009. *Global education digest*. Montreal: UIS.

United Nations Educational, Scientific and Cultural Organization (UNESCO). 2009. Global education digest 2009: Comparing statistics across the world. *UNESCO Institute for Statistics (UIS)*. Available at: http://www.uis.unesco.org/template/pdf/ged/2009/GED_2009_EN.pdf.

U.S. Dept. of Education. Institute for Education Services. Issues Brief, Dec. 2010. *Tracking students at 200 percent of normal time: Effect on institutional graduation rates*. (NCES 2011-221). Washington, DC: National Center for Education Statistics.

Vanderbilt University, Center for Teaching. 2010. *Motivating students*. Available at: http://cft.vanderbilt.edu/teaching-guides/interactions/motivating-students/.

Wallis, Claudia, Wendy Cole, Sonja Steptoe, and Sarah Sturmon Dale. 2006. The multitasking generation. *Time*, March 27, 48–55.

Washington State University (WSU), WSU Critical Thinking Project. 1996. *CT Rubrics*. Available at: http://wsuctproject.wsu.edu/index.htm.

Weimer, Maryellen. 2002. *Learner-centered classroom: Five key changes to practice*. San Francisco, CA: Jossey-Bass.

Weimer, Maryellen. 2009. *Tips for encouraging student participation in classroom discussions*. (14–15). Available at: http://www.facultyfocus.com/free-report/tips-for-encouraging-student-participation-in-classroom-discussions/.

Wells, Marilyn A., and Beverly D. Jones. 2005. Commonsense ISD: An empirical approach to teaching systems analysis and design. *Conferences in Research and Practice in Information Technology*, 42.

Wilkinson, James, and Helen Ansell, eds. 1992. Introduction. *On teaching and learning*. Cambridge, MA: Derek Bok Center for Teaching and Learning.

Winter, Dale, Paula Lemons, Jack Bookman, and William Hoese. 2001. Novice instructors and student-centered instruction: Identifying and addressing obstacles to learning in the college science laboratory. *The Journal of Scholarship of Teaching and Learning*, 2 (1):15–42.

Wohlfarth, DeDe, Daniel Sheras, Jessica L. Bennett, Bethany Simon, Jody H. Pimentel, and Laura E. Gabel. 2008. Student perceptions of learner-centered teaching. *Insight: A Journal of Scholarly Teaching*, 3: 67–74. Available at: http://www.insightjournal.net/ Volume3/StudentPerceptionsLearnerCenteredTeaching.pdf.

Index

formative assessment,
  active learning, 59
  definition, 80
  learner-centered classroom, 70, 72
  teacher-centered classroom, 80, 81
  techniques, 81-82, 91-92

G

games (*see also* active learning techniques),
  68-69
Gen Y. *See* Millennials.
Generation Next. *See* Millennials.

H

higher education
  economics, 22-23, 40-43
  monetary value of, 11-12, *13*, *42*
  social value placed on, 39-40, 128
  student demographics, 12-13
Hispanic
  college enrollment, 29-30, *30*, 38
  definition, 9
  demographics, 37-38, *38*
  educational attainment, 31-33, 38-39, 43,
  value placed on education, 39-40, 128
Hispanic students, 37-40
  academic engagement, 48
  achievement gap, 39-40
  degree completion, 31-33, 34, 36-40, *38*,
    126-130
  demographics, 37-38, 127
  educational attainment, 31-33, 128
  improving graduation rates of, 129-130
Hispanic Serving Institutions (HSI), 9
  definition, 9
Hispanic youth
  media use, 99
holistic rubric (*see also* rubrics), 88-89

I

icebreakers, 51
institutional factors (*see also* degree completion (B.A. & A.A.), improving), 108-109,
  109-112, 117, 119-123
  definition, 108-109
interactive lectures (*see also* active learning
  techniques), 54, 55-57

intrinsic motivation, 49, 50
  definition, 49

J

jigsaw group projects (*see also* active learning techniques), 66-67
Jobs for the Future (JFF), 125-126
journals
  active learning technique (*see also* active
    learning techniques), 60
  assessment tool, 85-86 (*see also* assess-
    ment)

K

K-12 reform, 36, 109-119
  college-going culture, 118-119
  high school curricula, 110-112
  Hispanic students, 129-130
  low-income/first generation students,
    110, 120-121
  standards alignment, 111
Kiewra, Kenneth, 92

L

Latina. *See* Hispanic students.
Latino. *See* Hispanic students.
learning communities, 50-51, 112, 117, 119,
  Hispanic students, 126-127
  see also student persistence; social factors
learning revolution, *77-78*
  definition, 78
Learner-Centered Task Force, 91
learner-centered classroom. *See* learner-
  centered teaching.
learner-centered teaching, 69-78
  assessment and, 70-71, 72, 78, 80, 85-87
  benefits of, 72, 73
  definition, 69
  features of, 69-70, 73
  student buy-in, 73-75, *75-77*
  students' role, 71
  syllabus, *75-77*
  teacher's role, *71-72*
  technology, 55, 91-93
learning-cell (*see also* active learning techniques), 63